THE GALTRONICS STORY

William Goheen

10   9   8   7   6   5   4   3   2

FOREWORD

It has been two years since we first published this book. We have been grateful for the way that the Lord is using it to encourage business people to fight the good fight of faith to further the Kingdom of God through their business and professional life. As you read this story, I believe you will be amazed at how difficult these early years were for those who worked with Galtronics, and although we don't cover later years in this book, they have not been without trials. Yet faith has triumphed over the forces that sought to snuff it out and the company has continued to grow, allowing those working with it to minister in significant ways. This recent prayer letter by founders Ken and Margie Crowell testifies to how the Lord continues to work. You will no doubt appreciate this fact more after you read the story of its early beginning.

Galcom, "Go Ye" radios, Mega Voice, the Galilee Experience, and the Peniel Fellowship are all aspects of this ministry. The Peniel Fellowship is a local Church that is made up of believers from various racial and religious backgrounds including Israeli Jews and Palestinians. This Church began as a result of the company.

The Galilee Experience is a gift shop and cafe located right on the Sea of Galilee which also features a tremendous multimedia show on the history of the Galilee. It has been a significant outreach of the company.

Galcom, Mega Voice and "Go ye" radios are aspects of an effort the company has had to get the Bible to illiterate people around the world. If you want more information on any of these, you can find it at their respective websites: www.galtronics.com, www.megavoice.com, www.thegalileeexperience.com, and www.galcom.org.

Finally, if you would like more information on how to get help in being more effective in using your business or professional life as a means of furthering Christ's Kingdom, please contact us at www.johnhallerinstitute.org. May your journey of faith be a rewarding one.

WEG

"...and ye shall be witnesses unto Me both in Jerusalem,
and in all Judaea and in Samaria..."

Christmas 2005

P.O. Box 790
Tiberias, Israel

Dear Friends and Family,

Blessings on you and yours as we all celebrate the Birth of Our Lord Yeshua! As usual, there isn't a sign of any observance of this special holiday in the Land where it all took place! But at our house, we are filled with joy and rejoicing in the knowledge that we have a Living Savior who still walks in the Land through the lives of those who love and serve Him here.

The year of 2005 has been full to overflowing with many activities! In April we hosted the International Galcom Board meeting. This ministry has sent 500,000 fix-tuned "Go Ye" radios to 120 countries since its beginning in 1989. Headquarters are in Canada with the USA office in Florida.

Also in spring, we hosted an International Sales meeting for MegaVoice with attendees from Ireland, Australia and the States. This ministry, located here in Tiberias, is sending forth God's Word in spoken form. Called the "Word in Hand," MegaVoice is now capable of 80 hours of speech, the total time needed for the reading of the entire Bible. This is a major breakthrough (a miracle!) and we rejoice in seeing all of God's Word now available on this audio device that has no moving parts and is powered by solar energy! Please join us in prayer for the Lord to use MegaVoice to speak the Good News of Salvation around the world to those who cannot read but have ears to hear! A DVD is enclosed.

We are encouraged for the future of Galtronics! The Lord has brought a new CEO to come along side of Ken in the restructuring of the company. Growth is a blessing, but also a challenge! Wisdom from the Lord is daily needed in order to move forward as a Kingdom company guided by Biblical principles. The new facility in Southern China is in the final stages of completion, with an "Opening" celebration scheduled for early next year. Prayer is needed for all decisions to be led by the Lord, for it is only by His

iv

grace and provision that this work has continued to grow for 28 years! To Him be all the Glory!

The Galilee Experience is busy these days both with customers and the mail order service. Despite the unrest in this part of the world, tourism has greatly increased, for which we thank the Lord! The mayor of Tiberias is interested in improving the area of the waterfront close to the Galilee Experience, so good things are happening. How thankful we are that the Lord has kept this place of witness open all these years! May the enclosed calendar be a reminder to pray for us in 2006!

Peniel Fellowship continues to grow in two ways: people being born-again, and babies being born! We have a very fruitful congregation with many young families… a blessing to all! There is a need for more space; we must go early to get our seat near the front, and so this is a prayer request. What a great time of praise, worship, teaching, and fellowship we share each week! The Lord is Good!

In the midst of our busy days we continue to thank the Lord for our family! Lots of phone calls and letters keep us in close touch, and we hope to see each one this coming holiday season. James and Ruth continue to live and work in Panama City, Florida. Both James' sons are also in Florida: Jason is now stationed at Elgin Air Force Base, and Justin is finishing High School near Vero Beach. Judy and Charles and five children are also settled and happy in Florida. Mikey, Tim and Angela are very busy with school and church activities, while the girls work fulltime and attend classes. Annie is studying Child Care at Broward Community College, and Lydie is learning at the Fort Lauderdale Art Institute. Hollie and Mike are enjoying life in California with their two children, Carissa and Devin. Our trip with them across the USA was a great adventure, and as Ken says, "We would do it again anytime!"

May the Presence and joy of the Lord be with you at Christmas and into the New Year!

Ken and Margie Crowell

PREFACE

A changed life: testimony of Gary Hull, Galtronics Scotland

We saw his car and the cars of others from the company in the hotel parking lot. Charles had been inviting us to attend but we were torn. On the one hand, we were really attracted to these folks and knew they had something we didn't. On the other hand, they were strange. And there was a certain stigma that was attached to them, these believers. Ette and I drove on by and returned home. But we continued to talk about it that whole Saturday.

I had first met Charles in Hebrew class. I had come to Israel from Nigeria where I had been a manager of a five star hotel. My mother had immigrated to Israel from England several years earlier and I wanted to spend some time with her and get my head straight again. I knew I was drinking too much in my job and I thought this time in Israel with a change of scenery might help.

My mother had left Austria right before W.W. II and had gone to England. She met and married my father even though she was a Jew and he was an Anglican. Neither of them were really into religion so it didn't matter what their background was. She came to Israel after my father had died.

After graduation from University, I had gone into hotel management and had worked my way up through the ranks as I managed various departments in hotels in England and Europe. I liked the life I could lead in this hotel management role. Everyone did what you said. All of the luxuries available to the guests were yours to enjoy as well. But there was a dissatisfaction as well. I suppose that is why I was drinking more and more. I had to check the inventory in the liquor supply room each morning so it was easy to open a bottle and have a drink. Then it seemed natural to keep drinking throughout the day.

Through Charles Cibene, I met his father in law, Ken Crowell, who owned Galtronics. I had mentioned to Ken that I didn't like my present job. He told me about the factory and asked if I would like to come and work for him. I had another friend who had emigrated from England and we had been thinking of starting a sewing business to make bags for cellular phones. This opportunity to work with a company which made cellular phone antennae seemed like a great opportunity to get a foot in the door. Working on the production line was really boring, virtually no responsibility. Just pick up a part and put it in, pick up another part and put it in, so on and so on. Gradually however, I was given more responsibility and it became more interesting. Meeting Ette, who was working as a secretary, made work much more interesting. As the months went on, we fell in love and were married; two Jews meeting and marrying because we worked in a Christian owned company!

As I mentioned, Charles Cibene continued to ask if we would like to visit the little church service that met in the hotel. After we had driven by that Shabbat, he had encouraged us the following week even more enthusiastically. The next week we decided to visit. After all, why not? We had nothing else interesting to do. What harm could be in it?

I don't remember a whole lot about the service except they had a visiting speaker who seemed to go on and on. I looked over at Charles and he just shrugged apologetically. Despite the bad experience, we were struck by how friendly the people were. Charles and Judy asked us if we would like to study the Bible with them in the evening. We agreed. After that, we began to attend the service every week and we continued in the Bible study.

As the weeks went by, we had more and more questions answered. I won't go into all of the details but eventually, both of us accepted Jesus as the Messiah. From that time to present, our lives have been eternally changed. Not only did I stop drinking but I had been given a new purpose in life. Now we are living in Scotland and working with Galtronics Scotland. Our kids have accepted Jesus as well. I don't know what life would have been like if I had not met Charles and begun working at that company. Certainly, much different.

Gary and Ester (Ette) Hull are just two of the people whose lives have been forever changed because Ken and Margie Crowell obeyed the Lord in their personal lives and in their business. This is the story of Galtronics. As you read, we trust you will gain a new appreciation for how the Lord uses people in the context of "for profit" business to accomplish His purposes.

Chapter One

Learning through Listening

When Gary Ginter introduced to me his interest in researching and preparing case studies of "Kingdom-building Businesses,"[1] I liked the idea. In fact I said, "I'd love to read them when they're finished!" For nearly 30 years, I've struggled with integrating my call to follow Christ into my business and professional life so I was open to learning from others in any way I could. But with more questions than answers, I hardly felt qualified when Gary asked me to document and write the first case. However, he persisted. Eventually, I agreed to give it a go. I looked forward to discovering answers to my own personal questions about how one effectively follows the Lord into the workplace. After fervent prayer for direction in selecting the first case to study, we were thankful when Ken and Margie Crowell, the founders of Galtronics, agreed to open their lives and business to our exploration. After getting to know them, I can say with confidence their heart is to serve Christ and further His Kingdom. I praise God for Ken and Margie and for many named and unnamed others whose lives make the Galtronics story the work of God's grace that it is.

I have learned much as I have had the privilege of doing thirty-one interviews, watching historical videos, reading other historical background and compiling the information to create this volume. I pray it will motivate and instruct others to see their business or profession as a strategic platform of Christian service.

---

[1] Definitions of what Kingdom Building Businesses means will vary. In the chapter A Tool For Integration, we introduce a taxonomy which seeks to better define this. In short we use it here to refer to businesses whose owners seek to further the Kingdom of God by running their businesses on Biblical Principles and to one degree or another seek to make disciples through relationships formed in and through the business. This may result in one on one Bible Studies, small group Bible studies, or other manifestations up to and including any and all characteristics that would be "marks" of what most would call a church if they looked at it objectively.

Oswald Chambers, in his little book, So Send I You, makes the point that all who know Jesus personally and call him Lord are called to live for His purposes. Jesus came to earth for a purpose which He has passed on to those who seek to serve Him. In fact, this mission of making disciples of Jesus is exactly what Ken and Margie were doing through Galtronics. In So Send I You, Chambers has a chapter entitled "Vision, Valley, and Verity" in which he notes, as God gives a Vision to His servant who wants to be aligned with His purposes, that servant can expect to be taken through a Valley of Humiliation before the Vision becomes a reality, or Verity.

Chambers illustrates Biblical truth through examples from the lives of Abraham, Moses and Isaiah. He writes "it does not matter with what the Vision is connected, there is always something that corresponds to the Valley of Humiliation during which self sufficiency is destroyed and every strand of self-reliance is broken."[2] This concept is a difficult truth to accept. However it is what those who want to follow Jesus need to know if they are to have their Master say to them at heaven's gate, "Well done, my good and faithful servant."

I have used this "Vision, Valley and Verity" motif to characterize the history of Galtronics. It became evident to me as I did the interviews that God was using the business and the people in the business to accomplish a great purpose. As you read this book, I am sure you will agree Ken and Margie Crowell experienced this "Vision, Valley and Verity" pattern. If you were to ask them today if the struggles they experienced throughout their Kingdom-building business were worth it, there is no doubt in my mind they would answer in the affirmative. In fact, they are indeed encouraging others abroad to do likewise!

As you read their story, I hope and pray you will be encouraged to explore options for how you might use your business or profession as a vehicle for bringing glory to the Lord and for furthering His Kingdom. The John Haller Institute wants to help you to achieve that end.

Can you imagine millions of acres of grain ripened for the harvest with thousands of laborers seeking to gather in the crop by hand when hundreds of huge combines are sitting in the barns unused? The grain ripe unto harvest represents those in several thousand people, ethnic, and language groups who have not yet had a chance to hear what Christ has

[2] Chambers, Oswald; *So Send I You*, Christian Literature Crusade, Fort Washington, PA; 1964; page 27-28.

done for them. The laborers are those seeking to find ways to communicate this truth. But the combines are businesses that could be used as vehicles and platforms for building the necessary trust relationships! The sad truth is many of these businesses are largely being ignored as strategic tools for reaping a great harvest. We hope by the time you finish reading this book you will better understand the potential of using your profession and/or business as a great combine to bring in the harvest. "Come labor on."

Chapter Two

The Early Years - A Vision Is Born

Today, the San Fernando Valley is a bedroom community of Los Angeles. In the early 1950's, it was still a farming community. It was in that valley in an Algebra class at Van Nuys High School where Ken and Margie first met. Ken was a senior and Margie, a junior. Through years of practice, Ken had developed an ability to take the initiative in building friendships. Because his father was an itinerant builder, the family had moved thirty-two times by Ken's senior year. Early in life Ken had developed an appreciation for a quote by Will Rogers and made it a guiding axiom for his life: "I've never met a person I didn't like." But apparently he liked Margie better than the rest because, having met her, he remarked to a friend, "There's the girl I am going to marry." He had good taste.

Margie was a very attractive, out-going young woman. She was a cheerleader and had many friends. With her parents and three brothers, she lived on a small chicken ranch near town. Her parents were very religious people and she recalls being in church often as a young girl. Despite her popularity and regular church attendance, Margie remembers feeling empty inside. She reached out to a friend, Jere, who seemed to have "something" she lacked. One day after school, Margie remembers walking by Jere's house and seeing her working in the yard. Walking up to her, Margie very directly asked if she could get to know her better.

"I see a peace in you that I don't have and I'd like to find out what you have that I don't," Margie said. Jere replied whatever she had that made her different had to do with the church she attended. She invited Margie to visit with her.

Jere's church, First Baptist of Van Nuys, was actually meeting in a tent at that time. During the service on her first visit, Margie remembers hearing about Jesus and the need for a personal relationship with Him. She responded immediately by going forward for prayer when the pastor gave

4

an altar call at the close of the service. In her excitement, Margie rushed home and announced to her mother, "Mom, we've been going to the wrong church!"

Her mother responded simply, "Oh yes? And where should we go?"

Soon after, nearly all of Margie's family members came to faith and began attending First Baptist of Van Nuys in its new location on Sherman Way.

Actually, Margie's hunger for spiritual matters was not unique at the time. There was a significant movement of the Holy Spirit in those years. Fifty thousand people attended Billy Graham's second Los Angeles crusade in The Rose Bowl on Thursday night, September 14, 1950. Both Graham and Boston preacher Harold Ockenga stressed that a return to Christian theism was America's only hope for avoiding destructive judgment from God's hand through the communist threat coming from Russia.[3] Whether the motivation was fear of Soviet aggression or desire to fill an inner void, the fact was in Margie's senior year, almost the entire football team and all the cheerleaders came to Christ!

When Ken returned for alumni day, he and Margie renewed their friendship. The day after Margie graduated from High School, Ken was drafted into the Army to serve in the Korean War and they put their relationship on hold. As Ken was in the service, from 1952 to 1954, Margie desired to go to a Christian college for Bible training. Her father was a WWI veteran and had transformed their chicken ranch into an outpatient ward for paraplegic WWII vets. The ranch was next to a VA Hospital that needed additional space. His plan was to change the chicken pens into apartments for the men, put in a basketball court and add other features to make it a desirable place to stay. He was supportive of Margie's going to college and very hopeful about this new business. She was excited about pursuing a music career as she was already playing piano for public events and recitals.

Unfortunately, just after Margie was accepted into Westmont College, the government shut down the hospital near them and moved it twenty miles away to Grenada. Consequently, Margie's father lost their investment in the paraplegic ward and was forced to sell the farm to pay off debts.

[3] "Excerpts from Dr. Harold John Ockenga's address on 'The Answer to Communist Aggression,' The Rose Bowl, Thursday night, September 14, 1950" as quoted by Marsden, George M.; *Reforming Fundamentalism,* Grand Rapids: Eerdman's; 1987; page 92-93.

The family moved into an apartment in Van Nuys and Margie entered Valley Jr. College and majored in journalism. Because of the heavy emphasis on evolution at this state school, Margie lost heart in her education and dropped out of school after one semester. She worked two years for Prudential Life Insurance Company until Ken returned from the service. They were married at the First Baptist Church of Van Nuys on June 12, 1954. After having worked in helicopter maintenance in the Army, Ken located a position in airplane maintenance.

After a few months, Ken decided to pursue becoming a game warden. He entered Valley Jr. College and was able to get a job with the Los Angeles Police Department. Through his police job, he developed a ministry of introducing to the Lord people who had problems. When Ken didn't pass the game warden test, he began to explore other career options. Because he had taken a course in drafting at college, he was able to secure a job as a draftsman with Aero-Jet Corporation in Placerville, California. Only years later would Ken and Margie realize how much God used Ken's failure of the game warden test to direct the couple into their life's ministry call.

One day in the late 1950's, Ken heard about a Bible bookstore business for sale. With a $1,000 loan from a friend, the couple purchased the small business and began looking for an ideal spot in which to locate it. They lived too far from the site of the original location for Margie to run the store and raise the two children they now had. As they prayed for direction, the Lord led them to a very attractive A-Frame model home just outside of town. They exchanged their present home for that model home, built a lean-to on the side of the A-Frame to live in and used the A-Frame for the store. The new property even had a pear orchard!

Around this time, the State of California was building a freeway through the area and was selling homes needing to be re-located at a good price. Ken and Margie purchased one of these condemned homes for $400 and moved the entire thing, piece by piece, to their newly acquired property. They re-assembled these better living quarters next to the A-Frame. In the process, Ken remembers moving the materials five times before it was finished!

The next five years, until 1964, were filled with fond memories for the Crowell family as they lived in this beautiful Southern California setting. Margie was able to run the store and raise their children as Ken continued to work for Aero-Jet and care for the orchard. During these years, God was teaching them resourcefulness, patience, persistence and determination, characteristics that would serve them well in the years ahead.

It was during this time another life-changing event took place. John Gillespie, founder of Victor Bible Camps of Arctic Missions, came through their area and spoke in the church they were attending. John challenged them to consider missions as a life call. Because John was working in Alaska, both Ken and Margie felt Alaska would be a good place to serve. They heard the Indians in Alaska needed dental care so Ken made the decision to pursue dental school and then apply for service as a dentist. Prior to this, however, Ken and Margie both decided to apply to Multnomah School of the Bible for more training before going to the mission field. They were both accepted. In 1964, they sold the bookstore, moved to Portland, Oregon, and began to take classes at Multnomah.

Ken, now 33 years old, was able to find a job as an engineer with Techtronix in Portland. He also decided to take courses at Western Seminary toward a Master of Divinity Degree. These were certainly busy years. In the process of their preparation, God began to re-direct Ken and Margie. While the details are sketchy in their minds, Ken remembers going to Margie one day and remarking, "I think I'm getting a call to go to Israel. This is the wrong way. We are supposed to go to Alaska. I like the fishing and hunting and all that stuff in Alaska, but I don't know what is over in Israel."

Margie remembers responding, "Well, that must be the Lord's will because I feel like I'm getting the same calling!" As Margie reflects on how the Lord re-directed, this is what she says happened:

> I think it started because we were studying the Bible all the time and we were talking about Israel. But I also remember buying a landscape book on Israel. It was all barren and quite different from what we had grown used to in lush and green Oregon or even in California although that was dry. But through this book and our studies of the Old Testament historical setting, God was changing our heart's desire and giving us a call to Israel. Interestingly, we also began to meet people who were Jewish. We sensed that this was a confirmation of the change from Alaska to Israel.

The couple began to explore opportunities with various missions agencies but found none. In 1968, no missions boards were taking new candidates for Israel. All doors seemed to be closed. Ken shared his interest in Israel with some of his associates at work. Coincidentally, about this time, Techtronix was working on a project with the Israeli Air force Instrumentation Division. There was a visiting representative onsite in Portland to oversee the work. Knowing of Ken's interest in Israel, his boss suggested Ken and Margie have Major Joseph Barnea over for dinner. They were thrilled with the opportunity and Margie remembers spending a great deal of energy to prepare a kosher meal. Ironically, the Major didn't eat kosher food. He seemed very stiff and uncomfortable but he remarked this was the first time he had ever been invited to eat with an American family in their home.

Ken, in a very up-front manner, shared their call to Israel. The major listened politely and then responded, "I don't really care about your religious feelings but we sure need good engineers in Israel. Would you consider coming as an engineer?"

The question struck Ken like a bolt out of the blue. He had never even thought about using his engineering training in missions. Going to Israel as an engineer didn't fit the paradigm that Ken had in his mind for "missionary." He remembers how he had to think about it for some time. He prayed to the Lord, "You mean I just went through four years of Greek at 7:00 in the morning grinding through all that class work in Bible school and seminary, and now you want me to continue as an engineer?"

Eventually, Ken went back to Major Barnea and told him, "Okay, I am interested. Can you help me find something?"

The major asked Ken for a resume and said he would keep his eyes open. Ken remembers dismissing the idea as being such a long shot it wasn't worth worrying about. However, Margie had a different perspective. She began to tell everyone they were going to Israel. As she tells it today:

> Our whole lives we have always felt the leading of the Lord through open doors. We have never pushed. If the door was open we felt our part was to walk through it. If it was closed we backed off. We sent the resume and then I remember at Christmas, our

last one at Multnomah, writing a prayer letter to our friends saying we were going to Israel. We didn't know yet how we would get there but the Lord had given me a peace that He was leading us in that direction. If you don't have that peace, then definitely wait. God may be leading you in another direction. At that time, we had the peace!

When the missionary agency door closed it didn't cause us a great deal of concern because we had a peace that God would open up some way to get us to Israel. We knew He was going to have to work it out. That is a wonderful way to go because it takes the pressure off. You don't have to make it happen. And when I heard the Major's idea about Ken working as an engineer it seemed right to me. I believed it was of God and so I began to tell people that's what we were doing.

About three months prior to graduation Ken received a phone call from a man who said he was calling from Chicago. His voice sounded foreign to Ken and he asked if Ken could fly to Chicago for an interview. The call was from an employee with Motorola Israel, a licensee of Motorola Corporation that made car radios. They were looking for someone who knew the American market and could help them develop more products to sell in the United States. Ken flew to Chicago for the interview and on the flight home began to experience a real peace that the Lord was opening the door for them to go to Israel through this offer. He and Margie agreed to tell Motorola they were interested to see what would happen.

Because Ken had been able to work at Techtronix as they took classes at Multnomah and Western Baptist Seminary, they had been able to cover all of their tuition and expenses and were finishing debt free. As Ken says, "We were free to go. We didn't really have many assets, but we didn't have any debt, either."

Very soon after the interview trip, the couple received a thick envelope in the mail. It contained an offer and a three-year contract for a position for Ken. All relocation expenses were to be paid plus the company would also provide housing with a refrigerator, stove, etc. The salary was low, about one third of the U.S. standard, but it was typical for what an Israeli would make with the same qualifications. They would also be given one-way tickets for the whole family. To top it all off, Ken was even given

Sunday off because he was a Christian. But Ken said "no" to that part of the offer because he wanted to make sure they were living like the Israelis they were seeking to reach and Israelis all work on Sunday. Instead, they would honor Shabbat, the Jewish Sabbath. So they accepted the offer and began to make plans.

There wasn't much time to prepare. The couple had to think through what to take with them. While in Bible School, they had attended a missions conference sponsored by Wycliffe Bible Translators in which they had been challenged to "sell all of their possessions and go to the mission field." At that conference Ken and Margie had expressed their willingness to go anywhere He led them and to take only a suitcase if that were His desire. As this call to Israel came, they decided to follow through on their commitment and it was in that spirit they decided to open up their apartment to other students and say, "Come and get it!"

Come they did. People were coming in the front door and leaving through the back with their hands full. Only two things were saved other than bare necessities; a sewing machine for Margie and a bicycle for their son, James, who had worked to earn it himself. Everything else went. All they had accumulated over nearly fifteen years of marriage was given away. Ken and Margie graduated from Multnomah on Friday evening and on Saturday morning they were on a plane headed for Israel.

For the next three years, Ken worked with Motorola Israel. It was during this time their vision from the Lord was truly born; that is, using a business to bless the nation of Israel through the Good News of Jesus Christ. Professionally it was an exciting place to work. The company was in a growth mode and grew from 300 to 800 employees.

But much more exciting to Ken and Margie was the opportunity they had to tell others about Jesus. Ken was the only American and the only Christian in the company. He was totally accepted and was a threat to no one. He came to be introduced as "our Baptist engineer." As Ken describes it:

> In my office I had all kinds of Bibles on the bookshelves and held open Bible studies in the evenings for the secretaries and engineers and marketing people. We just became very open Christians. We were no threat to these co-workers and newfound friends. In fact, I had a guy stand up in the cafeteria one day and

10

say, 'Hey, anybody want a Bible? Just go to Ken's office!' It was as non-threatening as could be.

Other missionaries we met would share with us that they could not seem to get close to the Israelis; that they were viewed with suspicion and as a threat. But working in the company gave great opportunities for witnessing in natural ways. Fellow workers would often ask us questions. And we were very direct with them. That's just the way we communicated, direct and to the point.

Also during this time, the Crowells became involved in a Messianic Jewish Fellowship group in Tel Aviv. Ken and Margie helped work with the youth group in this fellowship and met a young Israeli teenager who would many years later play a very instrumental role in the fulfillment of the vision. His name was Daniel Yahav. Daniel's mother had become a friend with another immigrant family in their neighborhood. Both families were Jewish and both had emigrated from Europe. But there was a difference. The neighbors believed Jesus was the Messiah. They had started a small group for fellowship, worship and Bible study. They asked Mrs. Yahav if she would like to come and she accepted. Soon she, her two daughters and Daniel all had become believers in Yeshua as the Messiah.

Daniel's father was not of the same mind. He had been a prisoner of war in Auschwitz and had survived the "death march" before coming to Israel. Fortunately he did not interfere with his family's newfound faith. Daniel figures in the story later.

In 1973, the three-year contract had been completed. The Crowells saw three options open to them: they could stay with Motorola Israel and renew their contract, they could seek a position with Motorola in the U.S. or they could pursue a teaching position at Multnomah School of the Bible.

During the three years they were in Israel, they had become convinced they were called to the land of Israel. Tremendous ministry opportunities opened to those who worked alongside the Israelis in a business context. In fact, the Crowells pondered how much more they could do if they owned a company themselves! Thus, a new vision was born. Margie remembers, "Ken began to think of what it would be like having more Christians in a company that had Christian ownership and management. The Lord began to give him a vision."

The couple decided God wanted them to start their own company in the land to be a blessing in the name of Yeshua but they still were not sure how or when to go about doing it. As a married couple with kids, they felt their first responsibility was to their children. Their son was now 16, the age at which Ken and Margie had promised him he could start dating. The Christian community at that time in Israel was very small and they were not excited about his dating non-Christians.

A second family matter concerned their adoption of a little Israeli girl. The U.S. would not give her citizenship unless the couple returned to the States. These family concerns led Ken and Margie to lean toward returning home. Also, they too had many questions about starting a business. So for both the welfare of their children and the need to "own" the God-given vision of starting a business, they made the decision to return to America.

While Ken and Margie had not wanted for anything in Israel, they had not been able to save any money either. Because Ken had an offer from Motorola Corporation to fill a position as an Engineering Manager in a plant in Florida, the couple decided to take that position and work there five years. During that time they would save some money and look around for specific business possibilities that would work in Israel. They would also get their kids ready for college and allow their youngest to secure U.S. citizenship. The Lord was leading. The vision was developing. They were constantly aware of both.

Margie recalls their years in Florida as happy ones. The Crowells were even able to integrate their interest and experience by beginning a ministry within the Jewish community in Florida! They also introduced a Jewish Bible Class into the Baptist Church they attended in Ft. Lauderdale.

As Ken worked in his new position and prayed for direction in terms of business ideas, he noticed antennas for Motorola's hand-held radios were not getting much attention in the product development and manufacturing areas. In fact, they seemed almost an afterthought in the process. He also noticed radio frequency (RF) antennas were not being given much emphasis in engineering schools. The engineers he was hiring were being trained in mechanics and electronics but not in the area of antennas. Therefore, they had to be trained on the job. Ken wondered if this might be a niche waiting to be filled. At last he took the step of faith. In 1978, he left Motorola and started his own company.

Chapter Three

The Valley Years

Psalm 127:1-5: A Song of Ascents
Unless the Lord builds the house, its builders labor in vain. Unless the Lord watches over the city, the watchmen stand guard in vain. In vain you rise early and stay up late, toiling for food to eat - for he grants sleep to those he loves. Sons are a heritage from the Lord, children a reward from him. Like arrows in the hands of a warrior are sons born in one's youth. Blessed is the man whose quiver is full of them. They will not be put to shame when they contend with their enemies in the gate.

Any who have had children know the joy and pain involved. First, during the pregnancy, it seems like the day of birth will never come. Then the baby enters the world and a whole new chapter begins. How fragile and dependent this new little bundle of life is, dependent upon parents, doctors and especially the Lord.

Life is a gift from God and is always lived in dependence upon Him. Unbelieving doctors will candidly admit they don't know how or why the body functions the way it does. In times when life hangs in the balance, medical professionals can give counsel and advice but ultimately the fate of the patient is in other hands. Some have called it providence or fate while those who profess no belief in a Divine Creator will call it luck.

Yet those who do accept the Bible as authoritative in their lives and who accept as reality the existence of a Creator profess He alone holds the ultimate power over life and death.

Many to whom God has given a vision or an idea or a dream about something He wanted to do through them, have testified that vision is born and grows in much the same way as a child; in total dependence upon the Lord of the Universe. They, like parents, do all they can to help

13

in the birth and growth process. Yet when it comes down to bottom-line reality they must trust God to breathe life into the idea if it is to live and grow.

This process is exactly how Ken and Margie Crowell have viewed the vision God gave them of using a business in Israel as a platform for ministry. They knew the Lord had called them to be His instrument in blessing the land of Israel. Like the builder, the watchman, or the parent mentioned by Solomon in Psalm 127, Ken and Margie sensed while they had a role to play, ultimately the outcome was in God's hands. That conviction brought great excitement and great peace. In the years that followed they would repeatedly rely upon that truth.

Most people think the "Gal" in Galtronics stands for the Galilee region where the Israeli headquarters are located. This is not the case. "Gal" is a transliteration of the Hebrew root GLL which means "to roll" as in "to roll over your trust onto" or "to commit oneself." The word picture can best be understood by thinking of huge bundles being rolled up onto the back of a camel so the beast can rise and bear the burden across the desert. The psalmist in Psalm 37:5-6 writes, "Commit your way to the LORD; trust in him and he will do this: He will make your righteousness shine like the dawn, the justice of your cause like the noonday sun."

At some point Ken and Margie decided to name the company Galtronics as an open acknowledgment and testimony of their utter dependence upon the Lord. Many times as I spoke with the couple about the history of their company, this topic came up. They would say, "This is not our company or vision. This is the Lord's. We knew that if it was to succeed and grow, it would be up to Him."

Ken and Margie likened their relationship to their business as adoptive parents to a child. God had given them a charge to raise up this business as though it belonged to Him. They were stewards of this resource. As events transpired over the years, many, many times they would need to roll their problems and concerns over onto His "broad shoulders" and look for Him to preserve the life of the business, i.e., this "child." One major lesson they had to continually learn was being in the center of God's will did not mean they were immune to problems. In fact it was quite the opposite. It often meant they were subjected to many problems unique to their mission; problems a business solely for profit would not encounter.

This chapter is called "The Valley Years" because of the tremendous difficulties Ken, Margie and others working with them experienced between 1978 and 1986. Oswald Chambers said experiencing difficulty is God's normal way of working: that is, taking through the "Valley" those to whom He has given the "Vision."

After receiving what they interpreted as positive leading from the Lord to set up this Kingdom-building business, Ken and Margie went through some very discouraging and increasingly intense difficulties some might say indicated they had missed God's direction altogether! Chambers' interpretation of this pattern is that God, having headed His servants in the right direction, must train them to trust in Him rather than in themselves. The only way to do this is to take them through the "Valley of Humiliation." While Chambers mentions three cases, the Scriptures are replete with examples. Certainly David could relate to this line of thinking as we read Psalm 23: "Yea, though I walk through the valley of the shadow of death, I will fear no evil."

David, in so many of his Psalms, describes and laments the trials through which he is being taken. But he always demonstrates his faith and trust as he remembers God's faithfulness to Israel in general and to himself in particular. He often would openly acknowledge his problems to the Lord through a lament but then would assert his confidence in God by giving a statement of assurance that his Lord would ultimately accomplish His purposes. As Margie often said, she and Ken knew they were called by God to do His work through their business. It would become a reality only if He did it. They believed to rely on their own abilities and resources alone would greatly undercut the possible results that could be achieved were they to rely on God's power for fulfillment of His vision.

In 1976, having left Motorola Florida, Ken formed an antenna company in the United States. The plan was this U.S. entity would then finance the Israeli entity as it developed. Ken had determined, as previously mentioned, he wanted to focus on the antenna market. A major competitor was a company called High Gain. Unfortunately, High Gain had selected a bandwidth for its radio antennas which the customers in their marketplace did not select. All the radios being designed and manufactured were tuned to a different frequency from the antenna High Gain had designed. High Gain had a huge loss and ended up going bankrupt. This loss left the door open for Ken and his new company. God was leading.

Before Ken could proceed, he knew he needed approval from the Israeli government. He and his attorney traveled to Atlanta, Georgia, to visit the Israeli consulate. Ken decided to be very open about his goals. Forthrightness had been his previous approach when he had been in Israel and he wanted to continue in like manner. Ken recalls the meeting with the consulate official:

> I looked at the officer and said, "We would like to form a company and we would like your approval to take it to Israel."
>
> The officer led us into a back room with a locked door and no windows. Then he said, "Tell me more."
>
> I openly said, "We are Christians and we want to go to Israel. We know it is sometimes tough in Israel for a Christian company to get started."
>
> The officer was very direct and asked me what I "really" wanted to accomplish in the country. I told him in order to explain, I would need to refer to the Bible. I took out my Bible and turned to the Book of Genesis. I briefly reviewed the events in the first three chapters and then came to Genesis 3:15 where mention is made of One who would crush the serpent's head. Beginning there, I continued on to other prophecies that foretold the coming Messiah. I began to tell the officer I wanted to go to Israel in order to help people understand that Jesus Christ fulfilled these prophesies about the coming Messiah. I also told him we wanted the company to bless the nation of Israel and we wanted to create jobs for people. The official told me to stop. He got up and walked out of the room. I wasn't sure what was going to happen.
>
> Before long, he came back with three other people and said to me, "They've got to hear this. Please start over. We've never heard this before."
>
> We all sat there for a good hour while I went through passages from Genesis to Revelation. I covered King of Kings and Lord of Lords, all the way through.
>
> Then this Consulate official looked at me and said, "That is amazing!"
>
> So I said, "Now you know my faith and my beliefs and why we're going to Israel. If I'm sitting at a test bench in Florida talking

to an engineer, I will talk to him about Jesus as Messiah because it is within me to do that. I can't do anything else. In Israel, I won't change. You need to understand that I will not be different. I won't take Jesus out of my life."

Then the officer said to me, "Well, I'll tell you, Mr. Crowell, it's not about your faith in Jesus Christ that we care so much. But we do need your engineering and we need your business. So we will support you. We will back you when you get to Israel."

Thus the Lord was opening doors and Ken and Margie prepared to walk through them. This time, instead of giving everything away, they took most of the items they thought they would need to set up a household. Ken asked a young man from his church to help him. This individual was given responsibility and authority to establish the U.S. entity as Ken was in Israel focusing on the Israeli operations. Ken left money to capitalize the U.S. company along with clear instructions on what was to be done.

Meanwhile, the Israeli government assigned an individual by the name of Benny Laneer to work with Ken as a liaison. His job was to "grease the skids" and help everything to get set up. As Benny put it, "Ken, my job is to make your company a reality. I am to walk you through government offices and introduce you. I'm to cut the red tape for you. This normally takes eight months but we're going to finish this thing in three months."

And, as a matter of fact, within three months they had cut all the red tape and received all necessary government permits. This definite and swift progression through an obstacle-laden preparatory phase was viewed as the hand of God, opening door after door.

One day as Ken was in the middle of this approval application phase, he received a phone call from his attorney in the States telling him he needed to return to the U.S. as soon as possible. He wouldn't go into great detail but something was wrong. Ken climbed on a plane and returned to find out the individual he had trusted with his money and his affairs had swindled him. He had used the contacts Ken had with Motorola to get orders and he had established design and manufacturing operations. But he had left Ken and Margie out of ownership and had used some of the new company's money to buy himself a couple of houses and a Cadillac.

Ken decided not to take the issue to court. Instead, he took it to the Church. Sadly, the pastors did not know what to do. Therefore, they did nothing. According to Ken, they were just not experienced in dealing with this type of thing because Christians who had legal problems generally utilized the secular courts. Ken talked with his attorney, also a believer, about taking the man to court. As he recalls:

> We were up until 2:00 a.m. wondering what to do. We had all of the books and were going through them, checking off these things and the monies that were expended. Finally I made the decision to let it go. It was at 2:00 a.m. in a coffee shop when my Christian attorney friend said, "Ken, let's just give him your coat. The only other action would be to file legal action." I knew this was what the Lord wanted me to do.

Ken decided to follow what he understood to be the meaning of Luke 6: 27-35:

> But I tell you who hear me: Love your enemies, do good to those who hate you, bless those who curse you, pray for those who mistreat you. If someone strikes you on one cheek, turn to him the other also. If someone takes your cloak, do not stop him from taking your tunic. Give to everyone who asks you, and if anyone takes what belongs to you, do not demand it back. Do to others as you would have them do to you. If you love those who love you, what credit is that to you? Even "sinners" love those who love them. And if you do good to those who are good to you, what credit is that to you? Even "sinners" do that. And if you lend to those from whom you expect repayment, what credit is that to you? Even "sinners" lend to "sinners," expecting to be repaid in full. But love your enemies, do good to them, and lend to them without expecting to get anything back. Then your reward will be great, and you will be sons of the Most High, because he is kind to the ungrateful and wicked.

By walking away from a lawsuit and relinquishing his rights of ownership to the U.S. company, Ken believed he was obeying Jesus' admonition and giving his "tunic also."

Ken returned to Israel and continued pursuing arrangements for establishing his Israeli entity with the help of Benny Laneer. One day, Benny turned to Ken and asked, "What kind of sect are you with?" Without any defensiveness, Ken explained he was not part of a sect, but did believe Jesus was the Messiah and God wanted to bless Israel through Galtronics as it was operated on Biblical principles. Ken reiterated his intentions and desire to respect the laws of the land but clearly said they would not forsake sharing their faith. Benny's response was similar to what others in government had said. "I'm not so concerned about your religious convictions, but I will stand behind you and your business because it is vital to the development of the nation of Israel." This conversation was confirmation God was still leading despite losing the company in Florida. God was with the Crowells in the Valley. Also, it should be pointed out the trust relationship Ken and Margie formed with Benny has lasted thirty years. So even in the midst of the controversy, God was doing significant things!

A major concern Ken and Margie had to face in Israel was fellowship with other believers. When they had lived in Tel Aviv during their first stay in Israel, the couple had been able to associate with a local Messianic Fellowship that had already been established. In Tiberias where they were now locating their business, they could identify only a handful of other Christians. Soon after arriving, Ken and Margie began to meet with six other believers for Bible study and fellowship. Because of his seminary training, Ken was asked to give leadership to this group and actually to bring a message each week. Here again, Ken and Margie realized how the training they had received was all part of God's preparation.

Gradually this group grew and took on more of the marks of a church. It is hard to say when a group of believers becomes a "bona fide church." The following progression often takes place: fellowship, Bible study, worship, more formal preaching, communion, more elements of community involvement and finally, more formal structure for leadership and accountability. At some point in the progression, one might conclude, "This is a church."

In just such a way, Peniel Fellowship came into being in Tiberias in the early 1980's, (Peniel meaning 'face of God' in Hebrew). This group of a few believers grew into a full-fledged church that ultimately met the full range of family needs for those in the fellowship. Even though "planting" a church was not a stated goal of Ken and Margie, they were thrilled to see it develop. It became, along with the business, an integral part of the whole effort to "bless Israel" and a major fulfillment of the vision. This fellowship grew in tandem with the business and together the two formed a broad-based community or extended family for its members, whether immigrants, ex-patriots or second generation Israelis who had been reared in the country.

In 1981, a young couple came to the small group meeting Ken and Margie were leading. Later that evening, Margie asked Ken if he had recognized the young man who had been wearing an army captain's uniform. Ken said he did not. Then Margie reminded him of a teenager by the name of Daniel Yahav who had been in their youth group in Tel Aviv nearly ten years before. At once Ken remembered the boy and made the connection. He recalled Daniel's father had survived Auschwitz and the renowned death march that followed it, later immigrating to Israel in the late 1940's. There, he and his wife had three children, two girls and a boy. Daniel, his mother and sisters all had become believers in Yeshuah as Messiah and had become involved in the Messianic Fellowship Ken and Margie had attended during their first stay in Israel.

At this time, while Daniel and his young bride visited the Fellowship's small group, Daniel was spending time in prayer and fasting, asking the Lord to give them direction for what they should do next as he was completing his mandatory service in the army. Daniel was sure God had given him a desire to work after getting out of the service rather than going back to school for university studies. They were in Tiberias staying with his wife's parents when they had decided to attend the newly formed fellowship group.

I'll let Daniel tell his own story at that point:

As we prayed about what the Lord wanted us to do, everything was wide, wide open. We were ready to explore all possibilities but I had this picture in my mind of working in a place where they opened the morning work with studying the Bible.

We were living in my wife's parents' house. My wife's grandfather had immigrated to Israel from Finland in 1947. He was a very strong Christian and her parents were as well. They were very supportive of our seeking the Lord's will and not just taking any job or going to school which would have been the normal step.

We started going to this home fellowship group led by the Crowells. One day after the service, Ken, knowing I was coming out of the army, asked me if I would like to come for an interview at his company. I said, "Sure."

I remember that first interview very well. It was 1981. The plant was very small at the time and had, at most, twenty-four workers. I found out they began the mornings with prayer. There were some other believers there besides Ken and Margie and they would all meet for devotions at the beginning of each day. It sounded right away like this was what God had been preparing me for.

I did not ask Ken what kind of work I would be doing nor did I ask him how much pay I would be getting. Isn't that the kind of employee you would like to have? Someone willing to do anything for any amount of money as long as you have devotions? I knew God was saying this was the place. I remember Ken wanted to tell me how much my pay would be and I said, "No. That's all right. I will wait for my first paycheck." It turned out to be base minimum wage.

As an officer in the army, I had been making much more. Also, the job turned out to be the dirtiest job in the factory. It was a plastic forming process. I would dip metal fixtures into hot plastic at about 230 F. It was nasty. But the pay and the job were fine because I knew this is what God wanted me to do.

My logic made no sense to a non-believer but to me it made perfect sense. An unbeliever thinks that if you get out of the army after reaching the rank of captain and you want to build a career, you need to go and study to get a university degree. An unbeliever would not want to work for minimum wage after making much more as a captain and being able to get something better. Even though I had a wife and we needed a home, I was so happy that I had found a company that started the day out with devotions and prayer.

But consider for a moment; if you sensed that God had given you an idea in prayer and you knew it came from Him and wasn't your own idea, and then you visited a company that fulfilled that idea, wouldn't you be excited about it? I was. I was happily married, young and trusting the Lord.

And so it worked out that because of a small group Bible study, Ken met and hired a young man who had been in his youth group years before, one who would prove to be a key player in the future of the business. Almost immediately, Daniel began to see ways to improve the company. It was a tremendous encouragement to Ken and Margie that God had led Daniel to join the Galtronics team. Surely He was leading them. But why the difficulties? Could God be in them as well? Shouldn't things always go smoothly if one is in the center of His will? On the one hand, God confirms His call and brings people to join the team but on the other hand, there's betrayal. The financial loss sustained in Florida had been a huge blow. In fact, that storm caused damage that lasted for years as cash flow and operating capital to get their business established became a continual concern. But even in the valley, God was faithful. Along with the challenges came victories.

Daniel Yahav describes those "valley years." As you follow, I am certain you will come to appreciate both the joy and struggle of watching God work in the midst of the fiery furnace. You will come to see that even the terms "good" and "bad" have to be defined from God's perspective. Our narrative continues with Daniel's testimony as he describes his first months with the company:

I enjoyed the work. As I mentioned, I got the dirtiest job in the factory. I would dip metal fixtures into hot plastic at about 230 F. and pull them out and dip them into liquid Polyvinyl chloride. You have to understand that Tiberias is a hot place. There was no air-conditioning there. It was a hot, messy job but I enjoyed every moment. Ken and Margie were great to work for. When I was still dipping the PVC and I was dirty, Margie came into the factory and saw me. She said to Ken, "Look, he is so dirty! You need to buy him work clothes."

I said, "No, don't buy me work clothes." My wife's Grandfather had a ministry of giving out Bibles and clothes so I went down and got darker clothes from him. I was very cost conscious.

After I worked there for a while, I began to see ways I could improve things. I loved coming up with these ideas. But almost immediately I got into difficulties with my supervisor who was not a believer. He told me to relax and to not worry about making improvements. I was starting to take notes on the process but he wouldn't tell me what the process was. He wanted to keep it to himself. I started learning my first lesson about difficulties of work places. Some people are interested only in staying in control but the fact was that the company needed some process improvement.

There was no inventory handling process, no record or good accountability of materials. The factory was doing assembly of antennas we called the "rubber duckies." I went one day to Ken after I had been there maybe two weeks. I said to him, "I don't want to do something I am not supposed to do but, if you want, I could organize the storeroom." The storeroom was where the raw material and work-in-process inventory was stored.

He said, "Great! Do it!" That's all the encouragement I needed. There was one room full of junk. I emptied this room out and started looking for shelves. Then I started collecting the boxes and putting them on shelves.

After a while, my supervisor came to me again and said, "What are you doing?"

I said, "I'm taking these things to help you."

He said, "You are disturbing my job. I know where everything is around this place. Don't touch it."

But by that time I had about half the boxes. So I wondered, "What am I going to do now?" I didn't want to go to Ken because I didn't want to go around my supervisor's back. So I decided that every time the workers and foremen would go out on break, I would walk out on the floor and take another three boxes. Slowly, they were vanishing into my storeroom. It wasn't enough for the foreman to make an issue over so slowly I had them all. Then I waited and took inventory.

The Lord gave me this entry-level job for this purpose: He wanted me to learn the whole process from beginning to end. He also wanted me to demonstrate servanthood and to be a learner. First, I learned the process of running the oven. Then I learned the storeroom. One thing led to another. Having responsibility for the storeroom, I started keeping a more detailed inventory. When we were short on materials it became my job to order them. I had never made a phone call to a vendor and I did not even know how to speak to a vendor. I didn't know what a delivery ticket was or an invoice. I knew nothing. The first time I called a vendor I was quite nervous. I made the call and after I had hung up, I remembered that I had forgotten to tell them something. It was a very small, innocent beginning. But this led to what eventually became a purchasing division. It was a real learning experience.

I found that Ken was doing everything from his office. This was too much. Not speaking Hebrew well and not being able to control things naturally made it very difficult on him. He worked very hard and did a very good job considering his limitations. After I had been in the storeroom for a while, I started working for Ken directly and the Lord took away my problem with having a supervisor who didn't want to improve the processes.

After a while it became evident we were having quality problems with our incoming goods. This led to the beginning of the first inspection department. After receiving the materials, we would do an inspection and only release the good ones to the floor. Prior to that, the rejects would often only show up after the product was assembled and the whole unit would have to be scrapped. The difficulty was tremendous.

We were producing many scrap parts. The foreman would throw the rejects into a barrel outside the factory. Ken would come to me and say, "How come we ran out of these things? I just got 3,000 of them last week. We shipped only 510. What happened to the rest?"

Everyone would be "whistling Dixie" as Americans like to say. This high scrap rate was absolutely terrible. Then we would get rejected antennas back from Motorola and I would try to fix them. I'm not even telling half of what took place. It was a very difficult beginning. We would look at ourselves and say we are such a miserable operation. This is totally ridiculous what we are doing. Even though I had no idea what a factory should look like, I knew what it shouldn't look like.

The challenge was enormous because none of us were trained. Ken had a bunch of people who were not trained. We had to live day by day. It was day by day also financially. There were always shortages, always problems.

Of course, I am sharing everything from my point of view. I was doing purchasing, incoming inspection, on-line inspection, final inspection, shipping and receiving. Eventually all of these became separate departments. I remember the beginning of shipping and receiving. We would take the best boxes we would get parts in and use them to ship our parts out. The boxes were all different shapes and sometimes they would be the wrong size.

I remember seeing Ken standing out there cutting a box with a knife and taping it to re-design the box. I said, "Ken, you shouldn't be doing this. I'll do it."

I started doing the packing. So now instead of Ken's doing everything, I was doing everything. But gradually we were making real progress. We were getting other people into jobs. By this time, we even had a different foreman. Later, we ordered boxes we had designed for our product. For the first time, we would order boxes with our name on them. It made life a lot easier. Gradually, the whole product became better. This was the beginning of the shipping and receiving department.

I am sharing all of this because, as you see what the company is now, it is important not to forget what it was. God brought us through some very difficult times. Some problems were of our own making. Others were from outside influences.

Ken built an engineering department and had the beginning of a business office. These were the years from the end of 1981 until 1984. In 1984, Ken took me out of the storeroom and asked me to do only purchasing. He moved me over to the business office. He was preparing me to become the general manager. Actually, he had told me a couple of years earlier that he wanted me to become the general manager.

At that time, the idea was so out of reach for me that I didn't do anything with that information. Then, in 1985, Ken came to me again and asked, "Would you like to become the General Manager of the company?"

I said, "Are you sure this is what you want to do? I am not trained. English is my third language. This company is doing exports and imports all in English. All of the drawings are in English. Everything is in English. This is a weakness for me. I'm not an engineer and as general manager I am supposed to be responsible also for the engineering department.'" I asked very frankly, "Do you want me to do this?"

He said, "Yes." He told me, "Because you know how to pray."

I said, "You are ultimately in authority here and if it is of God, He will provide the wisdom."

And so I said I would take the challenge. This is how it went. Ken called the workers in and handed over the keys to me. Then he said, "I am giving Daniel the authority to become the general manager."

And so it was. I had just turned twenty-six. There were maybe thirty-five employees by that time and I was shaking in my boots. But I stood before the Lord and decided the very first thing I was going to tell all of the employees was that I was a believer. This had always been a struggle for me. The employees knew I was Jewish and yet I was praying with the Christians. I had never made it official because it was an embarrassment. I don't mean being associated with Christ was embarrassing but being the only Israeli Hebrew speaker joining the Christians was embarrassing. The people were polite to me and I was also nice and friendly to the people. However there was always an undercurrent.

To understand our situation, you have to know the whole issue of Christians running a factory in Israel was a big problem for many in Tiberias. There were open attacks against the factory because it was owned and operated by Christians. These attacks grew over time. There was at that time open war and hidden war. Open war would be bad articles in the newspaper or blatant attacks against believers. One night they cut the tires of the believers' cars all around.

Parallel to attacks on the factory were attacks on the fellowship. During the worship service, rocks were thrown through the windows and several people, including Margie, were hit. Later the hotel where the group was meeting was burned down.

There was definite hostility against believers and from the beginning as the new general manager I knew I had to be open about my stand. I knew there was a risk. I asked myself how they were going to accept me in this position? Are they going to rebel? It was a huge challenge altogether. But I said to myself that I couldn't play games with this part of it. As I worked this through before the Lord, I was released and I felt free.

Right after I was named general manager everything came crashing down around me. In 1985, the inflation rates were running in the 1,000% range. If you were in an overdraft position with the bank, the compounding interest rate was about 100%. It was ridiculous! The company was deeply in debt. We also got hit with a significant quality problem; our biggest customer rejected a shipment. We had a huge shipment that had already reached America with the same problem so we had to scrap the whole shipment.

One thing that I began to realize was I was trying to do too much. What had happened to Ken was also happening to me. I was doing purchasing, shipping and receiving, inspection, everything. Even driving the van!

I went to Ken and said, "I feel like a man in a circus juggling balls but I've got too many balls in the air and I can't keep track of them all. If any one of these balls falls, it will be a disaster!"

I was all the time doing something just in the last moment to spare the factory. I felt tremendous pressure.

Ken was such a gracious boss with a good heart. He wanted to do something but he could not afford to hire anyone else at the time. None of our choices were good. Everything we did seemed to aggravate the situation. The company was in debt and was suffering from this tremendous lack of finances and lack of capital. If we ever did make a profit in a given month, we had to pay the banks on our debt. That ate us up and enslaved us to the bank in a shameful way.

I took over leadership as general manager for the company in August of 1985. By Christmastime, the banks closed down our bank account. That meant we couldn't write any checks. We still had a bank account but we couldn't draw money. We had to get permission for everything we did.

This is how we entered 1986, which was the worst year of my life. When the banks closed up on us, we had no money to pay the vendors. Initially, Ken had raised money for payroll by consulting with Motorola in Tel Aviv three days each week. But at this time, we had no money to pay payroll. We had no money to pay the phone bill so they disconnected our phone. When they did this, they left a recording so those who called us would know it was disconnected because of no payment. It was a very shameful situation. Thankfully, the phone company did leave one line connected. But we were in a bad situation to say the least. The electrical company came and threatened to disconnect our electricity. But as if this were not bad enough, things got worse.

In this year we lost our biggest customer, Motorola in Florida. This was 50% of our business which got chopped off in one day. The reason was poor quality. They had put up with poor quality for years but finally came to the end of their patience. On top of all this, we had pressure from the Labor Union.

The unions in Israel are troublemakers. The last thing you want as a business in this country is to be under the unions. Their strategy was to come in offering to help you. They would say to us, "Why should you have to argue with a worker when you fire them because they are not doing a good job? If we are here, you come to us and say that person is not doing his or her job and we will take care of it for you. We will fire them for you."

After the very first contact with them, I knew in my spirit this was spiritual warfare and I sensed the Lord was telling me we should not form any alliance with them. I said to them, "Thank you for your kind offer, but no thank you!"

Well, that was only the beginning. They went to the workers at home after work and they told them anything they could to win them over. They brainwashed them. They told them how wonderful it would be if the factory went union. They would make sure the workers get a dining room and this and that.

So a vote was held and they chose one of the workers to be the ringleader. It is an interesting story who this was. This was a person who was introduced to us by an agency that helps crippled people.

He was very crippled. This particular government agency would find jobs for these people where they could make a contribution and build up their self-confidence. Often these jobs were for little or no money; just something that would allow the person to sit there and do something. Sometimes it meant the company would have to modify equipment and set up something special so they could have something to do.

Anyway, we said we were willing to allow this crippled man to come in and work. We had a foreman who was a very handy man. He built fixtures and things for this crippled man so that he could work. And as it worked out, the man did a very good job and got promoted. We made him a supervisor. In hindsight, this was a mistake. The union chose him and he turned against us. When we found out about this we knew it was war.

The leader of the union came to me at the office and said, "I just want to let you know we had our vote and so and so is the head of our committee here. From now on we are going to do this and that."

We managers talked it over and said, "No way! We are not going to do that."

We immediately got all of the workers together and told them if they wanted a union shop we would shut the factory down. There will be no union here. Then war broke out. Actually, the union tried to shut down the factory. One day they brought fifty goons in off the street. That day I was lying sick in bed with a fever and I turned on the radio and heard that a strike had broken out at Galtronics. This was on national radio! I couldn't believe my ears. I said to myself, "You must be kidding! The one day I am at home and Galtronics is on the news!"

I called up the plant and indeed there was a big battle going on. Fifty men from the union were there. Thankfully the police came and kicked them out. That evening we had a meeting with the union leadership. I went to the meeting with my fever and everything. They brought in newspaper reporters and started slandering us, saying the company was a dirty missionary front. They accused us of doing all kinds of things against our workers. They tried to organize a strike so we ended up finding temporary workers which the news called "terrible."

After this, I fired the crippled man who had been elected committee head of the union. When the newspapers found out about it, they made a big publicity show about it and told everyone, "They fired the poor crippled man. How evil." But what can you do? It was a disaster.

Then somehow we found out that if we had a personal contract with our workers, the union could not come in. I had not known that. As I said before, we had to learn everything the hard way. There was a lot of ignorance. Part of the problem was Ken and the other native English-speaking employees that had come from America did not know the language and no one had told them what the law said. Even though I knew the language, I had no idea about the law, either.

When I found this out, I said, "We need to get all of the workers to sign a personal contract."

But to do it now, when everything was in such turmoil, would not be easy. So I decided to start with a few among the workers who were believers. Three of them signed. Then I went to the most open of the other workers. I gradually approached other workers as I perceived their openness. In this way, we were able to get almost everyone to sign a contract that was fair for everyone which was the way we had sought to manage the company all along. By the time we got to the "hard core" union advocates at the end, they had already lost the battle because everyone else had signed. They could either choose to stay with us or leave.

All of this was very difficult. We wanted to treat our workers fairly. But the reality was that we had virtually no resources to work with. Where would we get the money? How would we do it?

We had a financial advisor who was not a believer. He was a terrific manipulator. He could tell you anything. He managed all the time to get to the bank and get more loans and would keep Ken going this way. We were, as believers, in a bad place because we were dependent on him. The problem was that he was an unbeliever using manipulative ways to keep this place going. I didn't like it at all. He was in the business but he was not under me. The situation got so bad for us that eventually he deserted. At least this was one good thing that came of all these problems.

The union was rubbing their hands in anticipation and the religious orthodox were happy.[4] The bank was ready to shut the doors. The bank had been told by the militant religious Jews that Ken and Margie were planning to default on their loan and leave the country. They even threatened to have Margie put in jail because she had signed the documents as well. Because of this, Ken made the decision to never allow Margie to sign any legal documents on behalf of the company again. The bank illegally confiscated their passports and gave them back only when Ken threatened to report the matter to the U.S. Embassy. It was a time full of various types of trials. Half of our workers left during these months. The union came in at least three different times in the morning and broke our windows until all of our windows had been broken. They were making plans to once again occupy the plant and force a shut down through a strike.

Fortunately, the morning of the intended takeover, we had told the workers to come at 6:00 a.m. instead of 7:00 a.m. At 6:15, we shut and locked everything from the inside. By 7:00, when the union came to strike, we were already inside working and they were outside standing. We were like Jericho under siege. Eventually, they left. For a long time we lived with this fear. If somebody had to go out of the plant, he would have to look left and right to make sure nobody was coming. The national newspaper reporters came and wrote bad things against us. There was one famous article where the reporter asked, tongue-in-cheek, when the Messiah of Galtronics was going to show up. In the

[4] That the Orthodox Jews and the Union were working together to get rid of Galtronics was quite an event. The Orthodox are very conservative politically - what might be called far to the right. The Union leadership are far to the left. Many of the Jews leaving Russia in the early 1920's were communists who had fallen out of favor with Stalin and Lenin. Even though Stalin and Lenin were very anti-Semitic, they had used the Jews to get rid of other Bourgeoisie members before in due time they turned on the Jews as well. Realizing they were now on the outside, these Jews fled, immigrating to Palestine and taking their communist/socialist ideology with them. Much like Pilot and Herod became friends after Jesus' trial, just so these two became allies in seeking to get rid of this company which was seeking to further Jesus' kingdom.

national newspaper, they were mocking us as Christians.

You know, I am not exaggerating on any of this. In fact, it was worse than what I am managing to communicate. But in the entire crazy, madhouse situation, God was at work. He would provide a way for us. We were able to get out enough production to get by.

For example, once I received a call from an agent of the bank: "Tomorrow we are coming to confiscate your equipment."

They came with the police. We knew that if we lost that equipment, we would be dead. So we did what we always did in times of trial. We prayed. We would always pray to the Lord. The Lord gave me an idea and also caused us to find favor in their eyes. I explained to the agent about our situation. I told them that we wanted to pay, but if they shut us down, we for sure would not be able to pay. They said, "Sorry, we have our orders. If you can't pay, we have to confiscate equipment."

That's when the Lord showed me what to do. He told me to get the old broken equipment we couldn't use any more and give that to them. They were happy! They had done their job. They took something. At least this way we could continue.

As Daniel's testimony affirmed, God did not deliver them from difficulty but always brought them through it. Another example of a time when God provided a way out occurred when Ken was arrested for allegedly making laser guns. Apparently, the Orthodox Jews living near the factory had filed a complaint to this effect. A humorous part in the story was the police rode the public bus to the factory and then asked Ken to give them a ride to the jail. They wanted to fingerprint Ken, but he declined. Finally, the sergeant in charge, the only one speaking some English, made a deal with Ken to fingerprint one finger only. This would "satisfy the situation." I'll let Daniel continue to tell how the trials continued:

There were many other things that happened at that time. We were so short of funds I was taking loans from believing employees to buy coffee and sugar and things like that. I had this little notebook and would write, "Mike gave 20 shillings." I distinctly remember the day when we were totally broke. I went to find someone to pay for the coffee and no one had any cash left. On that day, there was one package that came via taxi service. It was some raw materials we absolutely needed to continue. We needed the equivalent of five U.S. dollars to take delivery of these parts.

I stood there and asked myself, "Where is this money going to come from?"

There was no money to take delivery of one box. I don't even remember what happened but that is how it was at that time. I do remember thinking to myself that to go further down is impossible. This was a totally humiliating time. Around that time I remember going down to the bank with Ken. They told us they were shutting our bank account. We came out of their office feeling like lemons squeezed with no juice left. Ken said to me, "Let's go get a cup of coffee."

I said, "I don't think we have money for a cup of coffee!" This is how low we got!

And yet God was there. He provided. We made it through. I would like to share a story with you to illustrate how God took care of us. I remember the first time we had no money to meet payroll. This was very difficult. The few workers who had stayed with us were very loyal and very good. We were concerned about them and their children. Again, this all happened the first year of my being general manager in 1986. I had to go out and face the workers and tell them we had no money for the payroll. Our hearts went out to them. We felt absolutely terrible about it.

I told them the first money that came in we would use to pay the line workers. After that, the middle management would be paid. At the end, the leadership would get paid with what was left. That was our intention and plan. Yet we didn't know when that would be. Then a miracle happened. We were three days behind in payroll when my wife's grandfather walked into my office and said, "The Lord told me to pay your bill. This company is too important to His work to allow it to go down. It must succeed!"

I said, "Are you sure? Do you know how much that is?"

I told him how much it was and he took out his checkbook and wrote a check and gave it to us so that we could meet payroll.

Praise God!

But the next month we were in exactly the same place. When I say we could not pay our bills, I mean this was after our pulling every possible trick in the book. But the bank would just say, "No, no, no! You've got to come up with your own money!"

So the second month we were at the same place again. We couldn't pay the bills. Once again we went to prayer. We had a day of prayer and fasting and several late night prayer times with the believing workers.

You know what the hardest thing for me was in this time? I could not understand why it was happening. For me this was the worst thing. It was not the risk of going to jail for debt or being slandered in the national newspaper with my picture and name spread all over the country. The worst part was I couldn't understand why God was allowing this to happen despite our best efforts. I told Him, "I came here to serve you. I've done the best I could and yet I can't pay the vendors or employees. This is total shame. This does not bring honor to You. What am I doing here and what is wrong? We do not have your blessing! Why, Lord?"

I was crying like this and repenting, asking God if I had a sin like unbelief or something else. I was trying to be very diligent with every part in the factory. We would not throw anything away. I inspected it ten times if something would be thrown away. I was trying to manage our resources very tightly. Then there was something that came to the surface about the behavior of one of our management. I can't give any details. Something was exposed which had been totally hidden. After it was brought to the light, the individual confessed and there was repentance. Only God knows if there was a relationship between this repentance and the eventual breakthrough. Even today when I tell the story, I am making an assumption.

But the fact of the matter was that a recovery started afterwards. This was a very important spiritual issue for me. As I said, this was a tremendous test because I was going through feelings of great shame. I remember it so vividly even now. I have this mental picture. I was at my home one day and had come in from cutting the grass. I felt I was at the end of myself. I could take it no more. I went to my room upstairs and fell down on my knees and just started crying.

Then a mental picture came to me. Call it a vision or a dream. In this mental picture, I was in a big building and I was in the basement. I realized this building was my life and this basement was my life's foundation, my faith. It was the deepest level of my life, my relationship with the Lord. As I was looking at this, I thought to myself, "Is it going to crack? Can it take the pressure?"

It is hard to put into words but this was so real and it brought me to the deepest point of my life, my whole being and relationship with the Lord. In this state of realization, I thought, "What's happening? Can I continue?"

Then I cried out to the Lord! And as I did, suddenly a sense of peace came over me and I had a deep assurance that God heard my cry and would be faithful. And you know He was always faithful to us, day-by-day, hour-by-hour. Not that I didn't have fears. Whenever a car would stop outside, I wondered, "Who is that?" Or the phone would ring and I would ask, "Who is calling now? Who is going to scream and yell at me about wanting their money?"

I didn't think I could take any more and I cried out to the Lord asking for His help. Yet, our problems did not go away. As I said, the next month we couldn't meet payroll again. But then into my office walks my wife's grandfather. I didn't call him or ask him. He just showed up and told me he was going to pay the payroll. He took out his checkbook and wrote a check. What was I to do? "Okay," I said. "Praise God!"

Then came the third month. We were still struggling and I wondered, even half expected, this man to come in for payroll. But the other half of my thoughts said, "No way!"

I didn't call him. But would you believe he did come in again with another check. Actually, I couldn't believe it. And do you know, all those months that we were struggling, I kept wondering what in the world we were going to do. For eight months in a row, he came in and paid the payroll. Then came the first month we could pay payroll. We had received some proceeds from sales and we had just enough money to pay our own payroll. This was the first month he didn't come.[5]

Having read the above account of the journey through the "valley of humiliation" of Daniel Yahav, Ken and Margie and the others working with Galtronics, you may be wondering why anyone would invite all of these difficulties by being open about his faith in Jesus Christ. Why not just keep quiet and look for "private" opportunities to share Christ? Don't difficulties abound in just getting a business up and going without adding to that an agenda of making disciples, starting Bible studies, and growing a church?

Having talked to these people, I heard them indicate they saw the business as a means to further Christ's Kingdom and not as a means to accumulate personal wealth. Throughout this whole time, Ken and Margie maintained their conviction the business belonged to the Lord and it would survive only if He so willed. On the other hand, if He did not so will, they were willing to accept that too although they always had a deep sense the vision would become reality. This attitude was Daniel Yahav's as well. All of them kept their primary focus on the Lordship of Christ.

David Bryant (former Chairman of the National Prayer Committee, Founder and President of Concerts Of Prayer Ministries and now President of Proclaim Hope, Intl.) made the following comments regarding this phenomenon of Jesus' taking his followers through difficulties rather than delivering them from difficulties:

> Andrew Murray calls it the "discipline of disillusionment." Jacques Ellul calls it "hope in a time of abandonment." When we feel totally abandoned by God real hope can finally come alive in us. What a paradox! Prayer in times such as these is the closest we come to the Cross in the Christian life, I'm convinced. It is a mixture of sweet desire and holy desperation, coupled with a great sense of our hope being deferred and our longings remaining

[5] This "old" man was named Kaarlo Syvanto. The donations were all made anonymously, but after Mr. Syvanto died it was possible to make public what he had done. Actually a "tentmaker" himself, Kaarlo came to Israel from Finland in 1947 and spent fifty years in ministry there. Chapter Five tells more of his story because of the role that God had him play in the Galtronics story.

unmet; not just any longings, but our longings for God's greater glory in us and in the world. We cry out, "why have you forsaken me," even at the very moment that we are laying down our lives for the joy that is set before us!

We are caught. We cannot go back to where we were. But we cannot in ourselves make things go forward. It is like being on a cross. In this time you are not alone. This is a glorious moment of re-birth for the servant of God and renewal for the calling on his life. Christ is there and with you, whether or not you can feel His presence. He is there for one purpose: to come and conquer you. Let Him. Then, wait and watch and get ready!

Is Christ the Lord of your life? Is He the Lord of your business? Oswald Chambers believed everyone who called Christ "Savior" must also call Him "Lord." Those under His Lordship must align with the goals and purposes of the Master. If you are called to business, it is because God has led you there and has given you the skills, aptitude, and interests to serve Him in that way. God has a plan. He wants to have His people called by His name, representing every ethnic and language group in the world.

We are in a war whether or not we care to admit it. This is not a war against flesh and blood but against powers and principalities in heavenly places. This war has eternal consequences whereas the marketplace competition of business is temporal and limited to consequences in this life only.

In my interviews I had the opportunity to speak with many Jewish people who had found a personal relationship with Yeshuah as their Messiah. Some of these met Christ because of Galtronics. God used Ken, Margie, Daniel and many others to accomplish this change. The vision was real and required faith to persevere in the middle of the valley of humiliation. In the midst of the struggle, Daniel privately wondered if his foundation of faith would survive the ordeal. Earlier, I asked why anyone would want to subject himself to this type of ordeal? But as our story progresses through "valley" and into "verity," the question becomes, "Why would anyone want to miss the joy of the presence of Christ in the midst of the ordeal, or of seeing how He works?"

We have referred to Biblical examples of the "vision, valley, verity" cycle, but the most telling example is Christ Himself. Why did Jesus give up the glory of His heavenly realm in order to come to earth and subject Himself to open conflict and ultimately rejection and death on a cross? Scripture tells us it was because of His love and the love of the Father. This example is also why Christians would want to utilize their business as a means of reaching others for Christ, because of the love of God. The best news is God does not call us to do this work on our own. Left to ourselves, our foundation might crack, to borrow Daniel Yahav's analogy. But God is with us. In our weakness, God's strength is made perfect (II Corinthians 12:9). In the process of learning to "roll" our burden onto the Lord, we can watch Him provide. Others, too, will note His direction and provision. And, if it doesn't work out just like we want it to work, we can trust Him to accomplish His will through what does happen. As an example, there were many events that occurred to indicate God was with the staff of Galtronics in the midst of their "fiery furnace" experiences. Eric Morey, another manager and board member of Galtronics during these years tells about one of these times:

> At the height of the conflict with the labor union, the union leaders tried to sue Galtronics. They filed 25 lawsuits claiming Galtronics didn't pay wages on time, broke laws, etc. Now, some things they claimed were true. Sometimes we couldn't pay our wages on time. But this wasn't a matter of malicious intent as the labor union claimed. In addition, there were many unjustifiable, indeed, false claims. They were basically trying to force us into submission whereby the union would run the company.
>
> We wrote some letters to a number of people, including some senators and congressmen in the States, some leaders of Israel and ambassadors. The U.S. ambassador to Israel at that time, Thomas Pickering, got one of these letters. Shortly after receiving this letter, he was at a cocktail party with the well-known head of the ruling political party. This ambassador mentioned Galtronics to this leading politician.
>
> As I understand it, he didn't make any formal statements about it but just dropped the subject informally asking, "What is this I hear about this company in Tiberias that is run by Americans who are Christians? I understand you are giving them a hard time." Something like that.

Well, the U.S. Government had just given a $25,000,000 donation to this party of Jews. So, for no other reason than that, this ambassador mentioned it to him. This politician went back to his office and said to the union leaders, "What are you guys, crazy? What are you doing? These Christians aren't even worth wasting our time on. Get off their backs!"

So the ruling party official contacted the union officials and they withdrew all 25 of their lawsuits immediately. Earlier a lawyer had told us, "There is no way you can win this. Just give up!"

He was shocked the union released all claims.

God has His way of working things out and He chooses to involve us in the process. As I conclude this chapter, I want to reiterate what nearly every one of the aforementioned believers who had gone through the valley mentioned. God wanted them to pray. When they prayed, He moved.

For example, in the midst of the legal battles, someone was led to pray the Lord would "confuse" the opposition. The answer to this prayer was evident when the judge reacted to the charges given to him by the labor union by saying, "I've never seen anything so confusing."

This response by the judge was an indication God had led the people in what to pray and He had worked to answer the prayer. As a result of the confusion, the judge postponed the case for another few months. God was in control in the midst of the problems.

At another time of prayer, someone in the fellowship prayed that God would allow their opposition to realize by their own experience the same coercion and accusations they had inflicted on the Galtronics people. The police actually tallied up several criminal acts committed by the labor union for which they could be prosecuted. After the U.S. ambassador expressed his disapproval of the way Galtronics was being treated, the labor union leaders had to come to Ken asking him not to press charges against them for their actions. God had "turned the tables" on them. Ken demonstrated the Lord's mercy by dropping charges.

There were many examples of God's grace in the midst of the difficulties. Galtronics received an office complex full of new furniture that had been purchased by an Orthodox businessman who had been fighting to get rid of Galtronics. This man had a neighboring business with over 1,000 square meters of space for his twelve employees whereas Galtronics had only 300 square meters and forty employees. The neighbor had fought to gain control of the space and had slandered Ken with the city officials who eventually, because of political pressure from the Orthodox community, had relented and allowed the man to have the space.

In response, Ken felt that the company should march together seven times around this factory building. By faith, they would sing and praise the Lord for the acquisition of the building. After this march, Galtronics was eventually allowed by the city to take over the factory building, complete with furniture and other useful equipment the man had purchased. But the city officials presented a stipulation for receiving the space: they wanted Ken to sign a statement he would leave the area after one year. Ken refused to sign and stood his ground. Eventually, the city officials removed the stipulation and let Galtronics have the space free and clear. When Ken and his people moved in, they found every office was full of brand new furniture. God had faithfully provided!

Still, the question arises, "Why would one subject himself to this type of opposition?" As previously noted, love and obedience to the Lord is the motivation. However, only those willing to step into the battle will truly experience God at work. Those who sit on the sidelines will never know the joy and thrill of seeing God work things out in such amazing ways.

God allowed Galtronics to go through a period where everyone knew it was only by His grace that it survived. No human being could take the credit. These years had been filled with more major frustrations than could be accounted for by normal probability or the variables of business enterprise.

Daniel remarked he often felt as if everything were working against them. At one point, when everything was so difficult in 1985, he went to Ken to ask, "Isn't there a better way? I feel like I'm climbing a thorny and rocky hill on a blistering hot day. The enemy is throwing down hell on us. Isn't there an easier road that we could go on?"

I am sure that there were many times in these years when the Crowells, the Yahavs and others thought of giving up and forgetting the whole thing. But they did not do so. Rather, they kept going hour by hour, day by day, month by month and year by year. They held on to the vision as they passed through the valley. They remembered that experiencing suffering and opposition does not mean we are not in the center of God's will. They remembered the Lord Jesus Himself experienced much opposition and suffering during His life on earth. They remembered when things seemed blackest, they needed to persevere because the resurrection may be right around the corner. This was indeed the case with Galtronics. We'll discover this aspect further as we move on to the "Verity" Years.

Chapter Four

The Verity Years

I don't want to give the impression that everything was wonderful when the vision was given, terrible when they were in the valley, and then again perfect as they realized more fortunate circumstances. That is not the way it was.

All of us have experienced both good in the midst of a predominantly bad period and bad in the midst of a predominantly good period. Let's remember that Oswald Chambers said if God gives a vision or an idea or sense of direction, we must persevere and not surrender to seemingly impossible difficulties. We have seen how God provided grace to the leaders of Galtronics even in the worst of times. These difficulties intensified their earnest desire to trust God to a greater degree than they would have if they'd experienced only good times. In 1987, a series of breakthroughs confirmed beyond doubt God had fulfilled the vision He had given. The vision became verity.

Actually, the major source of these breakthroughs came through what had happened behind the scenes in the valley years. Despite all of the problems, Ken had been pursuing some engineering ideas he thought would be significant. Indeed, they proved to be so. This investment of time and energy into engineering development in the mid1980's led to Galtronics being the major world supplier of cellular phone antennas in the late 1980's and early 1990's. The first major idea was a development in molding technology in the manufacturing area. Daniel Yahav's description is instructive:

Ken wanted to enter into the product line of molded antennas. This required an investment into molding machines and molds which was a whole new ball game for us. The molding materials and the metal inserts within the molded part which were made of

42

plastic were very difficult to work with. In the molding process, a cosmetically bad shot meant lost inserts. That was devastating because they were very expensive. For the whole year of 1986 we were "chewing rocks."

We invested in a molding machine and later we got a second. The molding function was always a bottleneck so we had to work three shifts. As we were inspecting the output from this area, we were finding that everything the molding machine operators produced, sometimes for the whole week, was scrap.

This problem was concurrent with the union problems and therefore the workers were already experiencing much stress. They were often not motivated and working twelve-hour shifts did not help. Actually, the molding machine operators said they couldn't do anything about the poor quality. They were, in effect, holding us captive because they were running the machines and we, as management, knew less about the machines than the operators. Because assembly could not get the parts out of the molding operation, the whole line was grinding to a halt.

Finally we got so frustrated with the situation that the production foreman, the engineering manager and I decided to run some parts ourselves. Amazingly, good products started to come out. Instead of 100% scrap or 95% scrap, we would have 70% good ones. It was still unacceptable to have 30% scrap but at least we had something to initiate change. The production line started moving again. Then we were able to say to the molders, "Don't tell us you can't do it. We've done it all night long and the machine is working. It requires that you stand at this machine and stop fixing your cup of coffee and stop going to the toilet and keep it going. Keep the rhythm. If you need to leave the machine, someone else should come and replace you.

The operators lost all of their tricks and excuses. Other process improvements like this began to take place. In addition, Ken had invested time and energy doing some marketing and engineering work for other new product ideas. This work gave us an excellent position in the marketplace as the only supplier of the very first cellular phone antennas. We had an advantage over everyone else in the market in 1987.

Although I believe Ken showed great foresight, I don't think he would say it was his management which made the difference. Rather, it was the Lord Jesus looking over us. God set the whole thing up. The beauty of it was God was already preparing the way out when we were entering the valley of the shadow of death in 1985.

In a very short period of time, we came out with a series of new products. In addition, our process improvements allowed us to provide to our customers other services which increased our revenue and decreased our costs. We had been selling these units for $.85 and the competition was fierce. Because of our poor quality and high scrap rate, we were losing money on every one of them. Motorola had become so frustrated with our quality that they had begun doing their own molding on the older parts.

But fortunately for us, they had not been able to make it work in-house either. After we had figured out how to make it work in our new molding operation, our sales agent with Motorola worked very hard to convince them to give us another chance. They gave us a trial shipment and we turned the order around in record time with virtually perfect quality. They were so impressed they gave us the business again. This new antenna sold for substantially more money because it met their needs and no one else could do it. Motorola couldn't believe it! They started to send us all their inserts. We would mold them and send them back. We charged $3.00 each for the molding process alone. This was wonderful! Now, antennas were flowing in and out and as they did, the money started flowing in. God had brought us through!

The following graph shows approximate sales numbers for Galtronics from its beginning to 1993. The breakthrough that occurred from 1986 to 1987 is obvious as the company moved from the valley years into the verity years.

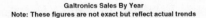

Galtronics Sales By Year
Note: These figures are not exact but reflect actual trends

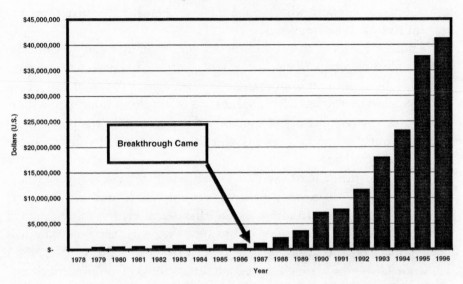

As sales increased, the company was able to reduce its debt and begin to provide employees with many of the benefits that before had been impossible. There was still a need to determine priorities for the designation of this money.

As anyone in business knows, sales levels tell only part of the story. Expenses, net profit and return on investment are some of the other key measurable factors that must be monitored as a business grows. Management went through struggles in determining spending priorities and though these decisions were often made on a consensus basis, Ken and Daniel played major roles. Current management testified to the difficulties in deciding how the newly available money should be spent because needs still exceeded cash flow. As management looked to the Lord in prayer, a sense of His leading in the decision-making became apparent. As Daniel said, "The credit all goes to God."

One thing I heard repeatedly from interviewees was the continuing need for a good marketing effort to select where to focus the company. I perceived this to be a real struggle for Galtronics throughout its life, just as it is for many companies. New products emerged. Many of these were products Ken and Margie thought would have an impact on their objective to further Christ's Kingdom. For example, they considered producing a small radio that would be tuned to a fixed frequency. These would be given out to listeners who would receive Gospel broadcast messages transmitted at those frequencies.

Another idea was to produce bread and wine that could be sold as communion elements made in the Holy Land. This production would provide jobs to agrarian immigrants who would grow the grain and grapes and produce the elements. A third idea was to develop a multimedia show that would give the history of the Galilee region and, in the process, tell people about the famous Jewish Galilean, Jesus Christ. I will deal more with these ideas later.

For now, suffice it to say that even though the company was now making a profit, there were plenty of current needs and ideas for new products that vied for funding. Again, these tensions regarding resource allocation are not uncommon in business. We shall see how they had great impact on the future of Galtronics throughout the 1990's. Mind you, not all of the struggles came about because of internal decision-making. Even as the breakthroughs brought success, the company still faced great opposition from outside forces.

One example of how struggles continued even after the breakthrough involved the physical building the company occupied which was a 300 square meter plant. To the immediate side of the plant was a vacant 400 square meter area. As Daniel recalls:

> We wanted the space badly and really felt we needed it. We were squeezed into this little space. As the cellular phone antenna business grew, we needed more workers. This was in keeping with our goal of providing jobs but it meant we were completely suffocated in this little space with nowhere to expand. Just a wall separated us from this other area. We were negotiating for it but then city hall got involved. The religious orthodox mayor said, "No! We need these 400 square meters to train high school kids."
>
> For a whole year this space stood empty. The city and state were committed to finding people jobs and we were the only factory in the area. But because of our Christian beliefs and the political pressure from the Orthodox right wing, the mayor was preventing our getting this space and thus was preventing our expansion. Because it was a Christian factory, he would not allow

us to grow. The workers had to suffer. We had no air conditioners; we were sweating like pigs. Then, after a whole year, we finally got this place. God demonstrated His faithfulness again and showed if we were willing to wait on His timing, we would see Him provide for all of our needs.

Despite the continued struggles, the years between 1987 and 1993 were amazingly fruitful for Galtronics, both in making money and in making disciples. When Ken and Margie had laid out their plans to the Israeli consulate official in Atlanta, there were three major goals identified: 1) to bless Israel, 2) to provide jobs and 3) to tell the Israelis about the Messiah.

By 1993, Ken believes all three goals had been met. Confirmation on the first one came in an interesting way. Of the three goals, this one seems to be the most difficult to measure. One way to judge whether it had in fact been fulfilled would be to have the secular Israelis acknowledge the company had been a blessing to the country. This is exactly what happened.

In 1991, Galtronics received the renowned Kaplan Prize. This award is a prestigious one, nicknamed Israel's industrial "Oscar," and is given to the company that has made the greatest contribution to the country during that given year. The day after the award was given, there was a headline in the newspaper in Jerusalem that read, "Galtronics Receives Kaplan Award for Blessing the Nation of Israel." But receiving this award did not come without its own set of difficulties.

Once again, I want to let Daniel Yahav tell the story in his own words:

From 1986 to 1988, sales grew from around $600,000 to over $1,250,000. This is interesting because when I took the factory over from Ken, I asked him what he thought we could expect from sales. He told me he thought sales could climb to around $1.5 million dollars. In my mind I wondered if this could be but he definitely had the vision for it. And he was right. We more than doubled our sales in two years.

By 1989, we doubled again and by 1990, we had more than doubled again. So, from 1986 to 1990, we had gone from $600,000 to $6,000,000. As a manufacturing plant, this was an unhealthy growth rate. Still, we were really praising the Lord for

His provision. During these years, we paid off our debts and renovated two factories. We designed new products and we bought new equipment. It was a resurrection. The unbelievable had happened!

So many people asked how we had done it. The fact is we didn't do it. The Lord did it. All of us involved in management knew it was the Lord. In 1986, we had held a midnight prayer time, not that we had some superstition about midnight. It simply was that after putting the children to bed, it was midnight before everybody could get back to the factory for the time of prayer. We prayed for two or three hours in the office. There were around twenty who were believing factory workers along with some family members and friends.

One brother approached me at this prayer meeting. His name was Pete Leitlin. He was an American Jew. Pete had a spiritual gift of prophecy. He had actually written a book about the Jews coming out of Russia before it ever happened. Now he suggested to me that we write a memo to the Lord. I said, "Fine."

He scribbled some verses and we wrote down a long list of things we were asking of the Lord. There were different requests regarding the business: good workers, good morale, good machines, good parts, good vendors, better products. These were all different items that expressed to the Lord the needs we saw in the business. One thing we wrote that night was that God would restore our testimony. Just as we had been slandered by the press nationwide, we asked the Lord to restore our testimony nationwide. We wanted this for His glory, not our own. So in 1993, as we looked back on our growth rate from 1986, we knew the Lord had answered our prayers.

But the most wonderful thing that restored our testimony was the receiving of the Kaplan Prize. One day in 1990, I received some government forms. With the forms came a cover letter in which we were asked to apply for this prize the government gives to businesses which make a contribution to the country's development. I am not sure who submitted our name as a candidate.

We decided to go ahead and fill them out. In doing so, we

tried to tell the events just as they had happened including as many details as we could give. We answered questions about our products and operations and sent these with samples of our product. We told about our struggles and our recovery. We even told about our struggles with the union and how we now had a profit sharing plan.

While I was working on the completion of these forms I kept thinking, "This is God's hand!"

On one of the forms I made mention in one sentence of our success being due to God's grace. One day, I received a phone call. It was a representative of the committee that did the evaluation of all the nominees for the Kaplan Prize. He said an evaluation committee wanted to come and visit the factory.

On the initial visit, just one guy came and surveyed the factory. After visiting, looking and asking questions, he came into my office and was reviewing his report and the forms I had submitted. All the time I was thinking, "I'm a believer and when they find out about my faith in Yeshua, it is all over."

Then the representative got this big smile on his face and, making reference to my statement about God's grace, he said, "What is this about God's grace being responsible for your success? You guys are not religious are you?"

So there I am, faced with a decision as to how to reply. I have always tried to be open, not hiding anything. I made the decision to keep that approach and to tell him the way it is. So I said, "Look, I'm going to tell you everything, even though it may be the end of any possibility of our receiving this prize. We are Messianic Jews and we believe Jesus is the Messiah."

"Oh, really? Well, this influences everything we do. Please go on."

I started telling him different things about how we manage and how we have sought to deal with the workers over the years. One thing that impressed him much was that I did not have a company car. Here I was, general manager, and I refused to have a company car because I did not want to take any money until we paid the last of our debt. He was deeply touched. He went back and gave a very favorable report.

Soon after that, a whole committee came and went through the factory. They didn't ask any questions and didn't get into the faith issue at all. After this, we were waiting. The results were kept secret. Actually, we kept the whole possibility a secret internally, letting only a small group of people know of the possibility.

One of the main reasons we did not want it publicized was that we thought, if the word got out, there would be people who would put political pressure on to make sure that we did not receive the award. As we had seen with the political effort to keep us from getting the space we needed, this was not uncommon. Often in cases where a believing family would try to rent an apartment, the landlord would ask, "Are you guys Christians?" After finding they were, he would refuse to rent to them. Christians are treated as criminals by many in Israel. So we kept it a secret. We wanted to be open but we also wanted to be wise; "Wise as serpents and innocent as doves."

Despite our efforts, word leaked out anyway. We didn't find out until later that there was great opposition to our being a nominee for this award. Yet, before we knew our opposition had found out and were fighting us, we received a message informing us we had won. This is a prestigious prize. They invite representatives from the company to the Parliament in Jerusalem and the top people of the nation are there to give out this prize. The main criteria in the decision is the recipient is to have blessed the nation. In our case, what made the greatest impact on the evaluation committee was we had taken in many immigrants and had made such a concerted effort to provide jobs for them. Over half of our employees were immigrants. Actually, this was one of the main reasons Ken had wanted to start a company, to provide jobs. Many other Israeli companies did not want to hire immigrants. They did not want them because they didn't trust them. We had a whole factory of them! Many of them were in key technical positions. They were designing products that were the most advanced in the world at the time.

Another major factor in our being selected was we were producing goods that were exported, thus earning hard currency and stimulating the economy. As previously noted, somehow the

Orthodox discovered Galtronics had been nominated and they went to the Selection Committee and told them everything they could to hinder us. We were the only company whose award was challenged for religious reasons. It was a close call.

After the decision was made, the award date was postponed two months due to opposition and political pressure. Yet the committee decided to give us the prize anyway. But then, before they could hold the ceremony, Iraq invaded Kuwait and Desert Storm broke out. Because of this invasion, the ceremony was delayed until further notice. From our perspective, this was an indication of the spiritual battle that was being waged around us. We re-doubled our efforts to pray. At last things settled down and a new date was set for the ceremony.

As the day approached, I received a phone call asking who would represent the company. I said I believed everyone in the company had made a real contribution and I would love for everyone to have a part in the celebration. Even though this was not feasible, a photographer was sent to Tiberias to take a picture of all the employees working in the factory. This was a special time for everyone.

Finally, the big day arrived. Several of us went to Jerusalem. Even my father was there. It was a special treat for me because he was seventy-eight years old and not a believer. But the day itself was not without its elements of spiritual warfare. Before the presentations, Ken and I were both on the stage having pictures taken. We looked up to see a procession of dignitaries enter the room and approach the table on the stage.

The Prime Minister was out of the country but he was represented by the Foreign Minister. In this group was the head of the Union and the National Bank. Also in this group was a Rabbi who was the head of the Orthodox party which had opposed our nomination. His name in Hebrew was Perush, a name that has the same root as Pharisee. As he came into the room, he was surrounded by a group of Orthodox radicals, dancing around him in some sort of religious ritualistic dance.

When I saw these men, I sensed a spiritual battle was still going on, even as the time approached for the presentation to be made. In all, receiving the award were eleven companies, all from different industries. Each of the dignitaries, in their turn to make a speech, had nice things to say about all the companies including ours.

Then Perush rose to speak. He went through his prepared speech saying nice things about all the recipients. Then, before he mentioned us, he pulled out another piece of paper from his jacket, opened it up and said, "But I think there is one company here who should not receive this award." He actually must not have known much about us personally because he mispronounced our name and called us "Gala-electronica."

But he launched forth with a long list of terrible things he claimed we had done. "They force their workers to enter the building through a low door so that they have to bow down to a cross. They force workers to say missionary prayers and read the New Testament. They give the workers 'magic' candy with crosses on the inside for their children."

On and on he went. There were six hundred people in the audience and the stage was full of dignitaries. This man is known throughout Israel as a man who attacks everybody he opposes. While he was still speaking, my father (again, not a believer) stood up and shouted at the Rabbi, "You're a liar!"

My father told me later he didn't care if he was on pension or what they would do to him. He was determined to let them know that this guy was a liar. You have to remember my father survived Auschwitz and the death march. As my father shouted out, the people in the audience started clapping their hands and yelling for the opposition leader to stop and sit down.

While this was all happening, the newspaper reporters came and shoved into my hand a copy of this same piece of paper from which the Rabbi was reading. It was like they wanted to see the blood flow. This reporter challenged me to retaliate when I got up to accept the award. Ken was sitting behind me and of course he didn't understand much Hebrew so he didn't realize all that was going on there. I turned to Ken and said, "We're in trouble."

But finally, the Rabbi finished his spiel and sat down and all of the other people went on and made their remarks. The time came for us to receive our award. One of the committee members read the report outlining why we had been selected. It was a glorious report. So the six hundred people in the audience got to hear the true story.

As Ken and I went up to receive the prize, we had to shake hands with every one of the dignitaries on the podium including Rabbi Perush and the head of the Union who, several years before, had worked so hard to shut us down. This was the same man who had taunted us saying: "We own banks, we own insurance companies, we own shipping companies and we are the biggest employer in Israel with over a hundred thousand workers. You guys are crazy. We are going to squeeze you. You will be gone from this town if you don't sign up with us."

It was like we were David against Goliath. Not only did David win but the head of the Union had to shake our hands. I had a picture taken of me at this ceremony with the trophy and in the photograph are the head of the Union and the head of the Orthodox movement. This picture is a testimony of how God answered our prayers at that midnight prayer meeting when we had asked Him to restore our testimony in front of the whole nation.

Not only did the heads of the nation of Israel recognize us, but it was also broadcast on radio and television. As I mentioned before, the next day in the paper there was a headline declaring we had received the award for blessing the nation of Israel. God answered prayer in the midst of tremendous opposition and, in many ways, used even the opposition to accomplish His purposes!

An example of this occurred through the newspaper's coverage of all the turmoil surrounding our receiving the Kaplan prize. The whole discussion of what it means to be a Messianic Jew became a public debate. Many said you can't be a believer in Jesus and a Jew at the same time. Those of us who were Jews racially and also followers of Jesus disagreed. There was much coverage dedicated to this, not just in the newspaper but also on radio and television. Prior to this time no one spoke about being a Messianic Jew. The Messianic Jewish movement was a quiet, under-the-surface phenomenon and very few people in the mainstream population knew about it. All of a sudden it was up there highlighted in the newspapers, with pictures and all!

I remember one picture in the newspaper with a subtitle, "Daniel Yahav, Messianic Jew, General Manager at Galtronics." The funny thing was this was a picture of Ken Crowell instead of me! This was particularly comical to those who knew both of us because Ken is years older than I am. People began to tease me about how much I had aged since becoming a believer in Jesus.

The beauty of all the publicity was that people began to read about the Messianic Jews up there at Galtronics. Then they would ask, "What is a Messianic Jew? Do they believe that Jesus is the Messiah?" It became a common discussion topic and led to televised debates and many talk show interviews. The exposure was really great and all of this truly confirmed that, by God's grace, Galtronics had been a blessing to Israel.

We already referred to the impact made on the Kaplan evaluation committee because of the many jobs the company had provided for the immigrant population. As noted earlier, the second major goal Ken and Margie had set for the company was to provide jobs, particularly to believing Jews and Arabs who would otherwise have a difficult time finding work. It is amazing that the Lord placed this goal on Ken and Margie's heart even before their return to Israel in the mid-1970's. By the 1990's, Galtronics had become the largest single employer in the northern part of the country.

Many of these employees were immigrants from other lands such as Russia, Eastern Europe and Ethiopia. We will let Ken tell the amazing story of how God enabled Galtronics to provide employment for these immigrants.

It was a miraculous story of how it happened. One day, two Americans came into my office and asked if we could employ a number of Russians who were settling in the Haifa area and who were believers in Yeshua. So many had come, there were not enough jobs for them all and they were sitting on the street with nothing to do. These Americans had become acquainted with their plight and, knowing me, came to see if we could help. In a few month's time, more than one half million Russians had come into the country. Most of them were highly trained engineers, lawyers, doctors and what have you. Many of these Russians were believers in Jesus.

Around that same time, I had received a phone call from Prime Minister Shamier's office asking if we could do something to help with the Russians. Now these two Americans walked into my office with the same question. I began to think that God wanted us to do something, but what? I wasn't sure what I could do. I told them both that we would try. Then I called Daniel and said, "We've got to do something but I don't know what we are going to do."

He said, "Ken, we need three things. First, we need a product to make that we can sell. Second, we need space, facilities to work in. Third, we need leadership.'"

A few days later Daniel called back and told me we had just received a big contract. That took care of the product. But we didn't have any money for start-up costs for facilities and we still needed leadership.

I went up to Jerusalem to a place called the Christian Embassy. It was set up to take a stand for Israel when the governmental embassies were pulling out of Jerusalem. Because Jerusalem was associated with a great deal of controversy, a number of foreign embassies relocated to Tel-Aviv or other environs. The Christian Embassy was started by a group of Christian businessmen and had grown to be well-respected and well-known in the country.

I talked to a good friend of mine who was an associate there. I told him I had never gone out looking for money before but I really thought the Lord was directing us. I wanted to be obedient. My friend, Tim, said he didn't know anyone who could invest in the startup capital at that time. However, he said he would explore some avenues and would get back to me if he heard of anyone. Margie and I returned to Tiberias without any conclusive leading. We said to each other we felt we had been obedient in contacting the Embassy and knew we had to leave the rest up to God.

It was either the next day or the day after I received a phone call from Tim. He was bubbly. He said, "Ken, you won't believe this! This is unbelievable! An evangelical guy named Casteen just called and said, 'we have a donor base that wants to contribute to a factory for Russian immigrant believers in Israel. How much do you need?'"

I told him I thought we needed around $100,000.00. He said they would put in fifty thousand and asked, "Do you have anything written up on the idea?"

I said, "Sitting next to me at my desk is a business plan. I'll fax it to you."

You see, when the two Americans had approached me several weeks before, I asked them to draw up a business plan and send it to me. I had just received it from them prior to this call from my friend, Tim. I faxed the plan to him and he faxed it to the interested investors. They faxed back stating they had adopted the plan and wanted to get going.

Then I called Daniel and told him what had developed. I didn't have as much as I thought I needed but I decided to proceed with what I had and trust God to bring us through.

We had the work and the money for the facilities but we still lacked the leadership to head up the plant in Haifa. Daniel said we needed an engineer who spoke Hebrew and Russian and was a believer. Where could we find such a person? This was really narrowing the field.

About two days later, Daniel was interviewing men for potential jobs. One came in who said he was an engineer from Russia. He was speaking with Daniel in Hebrew. In the interview, Daniel decided to witness to him and he accepted the Lord. So here was a Russian, Hebrew-speaking engineer who had accepted Christ! We were definitely getting the message God wanted this done. Actually, this engineer still works for us in the engineering department. He went home and his whole family was saved.

Daniel said he thought we still needed an experienced manager. Within a few days I received a phone call from a man who worked for the city in Haifa as an industrial engineer. He said, "Ken, I hear you are going to start a factory in Haifa."

He was an elder in a Messianic fellowship group in Haifa and he told me he wanted to work for Galtronics and would be willing to manage a plant in his city if we were open to the idea. He also told me he had wanted to work for us for some time but didn't want to commute to Tiberias. He had just heard we were thinking of opening a plant in his area so he gave me a call. God had provided everything we needed! Praise His Name!

This manager was amazingly well-suited to lead this team. Not only was he well-qualified professionally, he also saw his work as his ministry. He eventually developed a pastoral relationship with his employees and his workplace became his parish. He is a pastor and shepherd over his people as well as their boss. He is a very fine man.

He came to Margie and me and said, "Ken I want to have all believers because I want this factory to be a congregation."

We told him to forget it because we thought it wouldn't work. But he persisted and assured us the Lord had directed him and would enable it to work. It was a change of paradigms for us but we agreed to let him try. It turned into a beautiful operation. Sometimes when you walk through the factory you will hear all the workers singing hymns of praise to the Lord. It's awesome. It was wonderful to see how the Lord enabled us to achieve our second goal in this way.

These events point out that Galtronics was the Lord's accomplishment. It was also amazing that Peter Leitlin, the gentleman who had suggested a memo be written to the Lord laying out needs and hopes, had been given a vision of the Russian Jewish immigrants. This was the very group for whom the Lord provided jobs through Galtronics. Interesting, too, was the Haifa plant that had played a key role in the nomination of the company for the Kaplan Prize.

Ken and Margie's third goal was to tell the Israelis about the Messiah. More specifically, they saw themselves as supporting the planting of a local church. Ken sensed his call was running the business, not leading a church. But over the years a Messianic fellowship and evangelistic outreach were initiated so many non-believers heard the Gospel. Here is Ken's story of how God enabled them to achieve this third objective:

We came to Tiberias because the government asked us to target an area that was economically undeveloped. When we arrived there, we found only seven believers in the whole region. There were two midwives from Holland and a child psychologist and his wife. There was also a Finnish family who had lived in the region for some time and had a ministry of distributing Bibles and clothes. This was the family of Daniel Yahav's wife. There may also have been a few other believers scattered around the Sea of Galilee but we knew of only these seven. The Church of Scotland had a building and was holding services for ex-patriot tourists. In their agreement with the local government which gave them the right to meet, they had agreed not to reach out to the Jewish people in the region.

Actually, the pastor of this church was preparing to leave the country. When he found out I had graduated from Multnomah School of the Bible, he asked if I would lead services in his absence. I agreed because they needed someone. Still, I sensed that my call to ministry was to build an industrial base to employ people who could participate in the local church. In any case, that little church grew from seven to two hundred and fifty people!

This fruit of the growth in the fellowship was yet another testimony of God's working through these people to achieve each of the three goals He had led them to set. By the early 1990's, the valley had been traversed and the vision had become verity.

The "vision, valley, verity" pattern held true for both the business and the church it had spawned. I have gone into greater detail regarding the opposition faced by the business because this theme is central to the book. However, in the congregation was an equally harrowing situation of opposition. Believers were stoned as they worshiped and the building where they met was burned down. Had Ken and Margie seen this opposition as an indication they should quit, they would have missed out on God's amazing works. When the little fledgling church was struggling to find a place to meet in light of this persecution, it was a small fellowship of Arab believers in a village miles away who reached out to them. This kindness demonstrated unity in the body of Christ that transcended racial barriers which have inflamed hatred and dissension for years. This spirit of unity and love in Christ set a bold and obvious example and gave evidence to the power of the Gospel to bridge chasms now centuries old.

In conclusion, I pose a question to you, the reader. Why would you follow a God who calls you to risk your assets at least, and your life at most, to follow Him in starting and growing a Kingdom-building business? Given the inherent risk of business, why add the dimension of using the business to make disciples? In discussing this concept with Ken Crowell, he issued a caution to me:

> Bill, don't encourage people to get into this in order to make money. They may make money. They may lose money. What they need to focus on is listening to the Lord's voice. As they seek to know God's will and if they are committed to doing what He calls them to do, He will definitely meet their needs. Wherever they are in the U.S. or in Israel, walking with Jesus is all that matters. If God gives you a heart and gifts for running a business, that business can be used in a mighty way to bring glory to God and to further His Kingdom. Every one of the original apostles died a martyr's death. But to see God answer prayer after prayer and to see His demonstrated faithfulness in the midst of trials are great blessings.

Perhaps the more urgent question is why would anyone want to miss out on the blessings with or without the trials? Had Ken and Margie chosen to stick with their Christian bookstore in a Northern California pear grove, God may have raised up someone else to do the job that needed to be done in Israel. Thankfully, they followed the leading He gave. I trust this account has shown the extent to which many lives were enriched, including Ken and Margie's, because of their obedience.

It is important to note that throughout this process of walking with the Lord, trials occurred. Scriptures are replete with warnings that Christian suffering is both essential and unavoidable. God gives a vision and fulfills it but not without struggles and trials. Far from being a sign God is not leading, opposition and trials may indicate one is in the center of God's will.

In John 12: 24, 25, Jesus taught his disciples "...unless a kernel of wheat falls to the ground and dies, it remains only a single seed. But if it dies, it produces many seeds."

We have seen how Ken and Margie had to recommit their way unto the Lord and allow their dreams and aspirations to "die" by living in the faith that God could accomplish His will even though, from a human point of view, all seemed to die. We have seen how God brought them through trial after trial. Unfortunately, time and space do not allow us to go into the many fruits that came forth from the seed of faith demonstrated by Ken and Margie as they were faithful to trust God in the times when Galtronics seemed about to die.

Before completing this chapter on the verity years, I want to describe some other initiatives that grew out of the main business of Galtronics. In order to be successful, a business must focus on a core mission. Often, in the course of fulfilling that mission, other ideas surface which deserve pursuit yet need to be structured so as not to undermine and confuse those working in the core business. A difficult question business people should ask repeatedly is how do we structure this effort?

The Crowells and others working with them had many ideas that were worth pursuing over the years. Some fell within the electronics area while others did not. In order to manage these others, a parent company was established called the Gal Group Christian Industries. A number of entities were started under this umbrella organization. For instance, GalCom made and sold fixed tuned radios. Megavoice designed and produced other electronics devices used to spread the Gospel and Bibles. Galadon produced and sold communion products and was started with the intention of providing jobs for some of the more than ten thousand Ethiopian Jews who had immigrated to Israel.

One entity that developed in the late 1980's was called "The Galilee Experience." Led by Eric Morey, a manager with Galtronics, this for-profit organization had as a main goal the development and use of a twenty-six projector multimedia show telling the history of the Galilee region. It focused on key Galileans who have changed history, particularly Jesus Christ. This show was a means of outreach to tourists visiting Tiberias. While a gift shop, cafeteria and bookstore were operated as other sources of income, the slide show itself became a source of income. The show was so well-received, more and more people came to see it. The Israeli Army actually had their recruits watch the presentation for orientation purposes! The seed was bringing forth life.

If a business is to be used as a platform for furthering Christ's Kingdom, ownership must recognize the real owner is the Lord Jesus Christ. He is the essence of creativity and there is no limit to how He might lead those who are open to that leading. At the same time, business leaders are called to follow good principles of business. Ken is a very creative leader and the Lord has given him many ideas for ways to carry out ministry in business. More often than not, if his ideas did not fit the Galtronic's business strategy, a new business was spun off. Each new business required cash to support it until it got up and going.

Resource allocation is a critical element. Within a business, there are often more ideas than available dollars to fund them. Successful businesses must exercise discretion in investment of resources. As we read earlier, Galtronics sought to use business to reach people for Christ. Still, this disciple-making objective did not negate the need for the couple to use good business practices in the management of their Kingdom-building business. But as their company grew, so did the challenges of good management.

A single entrepreneur who begins and runs a business tends to sort out opportunities and personally make investment decisions. As the business grows and management is added, communication and decision-making become more complicated. Then, if other stockholders come on the scene, they may desire input. At some point, a formal Board of Directors and a more structured marketing and strategic planning process may be put in place. As the company grows and leadership changes hands, the decision-making process continues to evolve from its initial individual control to a team concept. If not properly managed, the process of making decisions can become rife with tension. The good news is God is able to accomplish His purposes in each and every phase of a company's life cycle!

In the early days of Galtronics, Ken and Margie made most decisions themselves. In the 1980's a Board of Directors was developed, composed of key managers of various departments or business units within the Gal Group. The members of this group knew one another very well and worked well together in order to tackle issues. Because Ken was still on the scene, he was able to resolve conflicts that occurred. As the business grew, mechanisms were needed to help insure that team members could accomplish more working together than working alone.

Throughout the 1990's and into the first decade of the 21st Century, Ken and Margie have sought to be obedient to the Lord as they used their business to further Christ's Kingdom. They will be the first to admit there have been many struggles. They have made many mistakes and learned many lessons. There have been growing times and pruning times as they sought to abide in the vine so they could bear more fruit (John 15). They would also be the first to say that God may lead others differently than He has led them. Yet if you are interested in business or have experience in business and have a desire to follow Jesus as a disciple-maker, Ken and Margie would cheer you on and encourage you to seek to integrate your business activities into Christ's plan of World Evangelization.

The John Haller Institute is committed to helping business people be more effective in this integration. In Chapter Six, we will share a tool with you to help in your thinking about how best to integrate business and evangelization. But before we get to that, we want to insert another story. This is the story of Kaarlo Syvanto, the grandfather of Daniel Yahav's wife and the man who stepped in as the "angel" who made payroll at such a critical time in the history of Galtronics.

Chapter Five

Kaarlo Syvanto[6]

In November 1927, Kaarlo Syvanto was accepted as an apprentice at the office of the Finish Railroad Traffic Supervisor in Mikkeli, Finland.[7] He had had what he called a "difficult and loveless childhood" which he regarded as a bad dream. His mother died at the age of twenty when Kaarlo was only eight months old and his father soon re-married. Unfortunately, his stepmother was antagonistic. Before he had finished his high school years, Kaarlo left home and borrowed money for a new suit of clothes that would allow him to look presentable for an interview with the railroad stationmaster. Thankfully, the stationmaster saw potential in the boy and accepted him into the training program.[8]

Kaarlo graduated in the spring of 1929, took the oath of office and received his first assignment into the 7th Traffic Division at the railroad.[9] In recalling those years of study, Kaarlo said he could see the clear guidance of God even though at the time he didn't have a personal relationship with Him.[10]

The depression years began in 1929 and work was hard to find. Having completed the training in the railroad apprenticeship program meant Kaarlo was assured a job which would not have been the case had he gone on to attend university as he had desired. Kaarlo later came to faith but expressed belief that the Lord had been looking after him beforehand. He attributed God's hand in his life as a direct answer to his devout mother's prayers for her small son.

[6] This chapter is taken largely from the book *Kaarlo Syvanto – Pioneer, Forty Years In Israel*, written and published by Unto Kunnas. This book is available through the John Haller Institute and can be obtained through their web site: www.johnhallerinstitute.org.
[7] Ibid, page 2.
[8] Ibid, page 1.
[9] Ibid, page 3.
[10] Ibid, page 3.

Kaarlo's first assignment was as an assistant station manager at a remote station that had a local lumber mill as a primary customer. On his first day at the station, the manager of this large lumber company came and greeted Kaarlo.

"Welcome to our neighborhood, Mr. Syvanto! Our factory club has an interesting social evening on Sundays. The station officials are usually there with us. We hope that you, too, will come and enjoy yourself there. We always have good relations with the folks at the station. We take care of your electric bills and we don't even bother ever to read your meter! And since we have plenty of timber, just tell us where your woodshed is. Firewood already chopped will be brought there. And if there is anything else you need, the factory has resources to help you."[11]

Kaarlo said he sensed something was not quite right and this thought became more evident when he visited the factory club and found the men were all drinking heavily and leading a fast life. He came to find out everyone on the station staff was being bribed by the lumber company with sums exceeding their railroad salaries.

Kaarlo had become a Christian and felt he must take a stand against this practice. As he became more familiar with the operations, he discovered the lumber company was paying about 30,000 Finnish marks in bribes but the state was losing more than 3,000,000 marks in revenues as station staff were falsifying bills of lading and overloading railroad cars. The bribes were a good "business investment" that gave the company an enormous profit.

In his biography, Kaarlo commented on his struggle in this situation:

> It wasn't easy to be the only oath-keeping Christian but my own responsibilities were immediately clear to me. Satan was intimidating me; "If you act like an undercover policeman, exposing the scandalous irregularities of so many men, are you aware of the consequences and cost of doing this? Even if you won't take bribes yourself, surely you know how to close your eyes when you don't want to see something. Just stick to your own business and dispatch the trains on time!"
>
> I understood my responsibilities and an hour before the next bill of lading was to be ready, I took a notebook and pencil. I

---

[11] Ibid, page 5.

went from freight car to freight car and inspected each one containing lumber. The bills of lading were not correct at all. I made my own entries for the separate grades of lumber and their weights. My results were altogether different from those entered on the bill of lading.

I then noticed another kind of fraud. At the center of a car were placed some prime, planed planks for export, on top of which were placed rough, un-planed planks which provided at the same time a roof for that car. The entry on the bill of lading indicated the freight was defective lumber which was transported by rail at a lower rate.

Kaarlo made the corrections to the bill of lading as to content but he could not verify the weight because the station had no scale. He called the station nearby where the cars were being weighed and asked about what types of weights they were finding on the cars from his station. The answer didn't surprise him.

"We are getting incredible loads from your station! In the small H cars whose capacity is ten tons, we are seeing loads of almost twenty tons. The regulations permit an overage of 10%. There is a danger the axles on these cars may break!"

Kaarlo told him he was absolutely right. He told him all overweight cars should be reloaded and the bill for the work sent to the customer.

When the lumber company received the freight and handling bills, the director approached Kaarlo and tried to bribe him again. He would not be bribed. He ended up exposing the whole affair. Eventually Kaarlo left that station. Four or five years later, he visited the village and inquired of another believer as to what had been happening since his departure. Her answer, he said, gave him a start.

"The stationmaster died soon after you left and the lumber company went bankrupt. In the bankruptcy, the lumber company manager lost everything he owned, even his own house, because in trying to avoid personal property taxes, he had listed his home as business property. Everything was sold at a foreclosure sale." Kaarlo went on to remark:

Wrongdoing never pays. Our Lord tells us in His Word if we surrender something for His Name's sake, we will receive back a hundred-fold. I lost perhaps 10,000 marks not taking bribes as my conscience is firmly fixed in God. How much is one hundred times 10,000? A million! From this time on, God's remarkable blessings have accompanied me in respect to financial matters.

I was stationed at Kintaus near Jyvaskyla shortly before the outset of World War II. I wanted to buy a small lakeshore lot and build a cabin so that after a difficult night shift I could go there to relax, fish and rest. The man with whom I was dealing told me he wouldn't sell a lot but instead would sell the whole farm. Almost against my will, he convinced me to buy a 52 hectare (128 acre) farm, of which two hectares had been cultivated. The farm included 800 meters of good, sandy lakeshore. The deal contained land and buildings. This happened in the summer of 1939, several months before the outbreak of World War II.

The cooperative credit bank granted me a loan of 100,000 marks at six percent interest to be paid in ten years. What we had in savings covered the documentary stamp, taxes and other expenses. In order to cut down on the size of the bank loan, I sent a forester to our forest to mark some trees to be cut for firewood. To my great surprise, the harvest of logs was many times greater than I had expected.

When the war was threatening our nation, the price of firewood increased so much during those months of that year that the balance of our mortgage was paid off! From the farm we received many times more than what I lost because I wanted to be a Christian and an honest state official at the Haukivouri station when I had turned down the bribe.[12]

Also on the town council was a man who had a hostile attitude toward believers. He knew I was a Christian and he was annoyed I had so many logs for sale. Other landowners didn't want to cut up their surplus because the demand for logs wasn't normally very great in times of peace. This official obtained a state mandate prohibiting me from cutting down trees in my forest in the future.

As war broke out, all owners of forests were required to have trees cut down and sold for a low price dictated by the government. But according to the state mandate, our forest was effectively

[12] Ibid, page 10-19.

"locked." I didn't have to cut down a single cubic meter of logs!

This brief snapshot provides a picture of the type of man Kaarlo was. He loved Christ and sensed a call to minister for Him in his job. He was able years later to understand how God could be taking Galtronics through difficult times because he himself had experienced them. He made the following statement:

> When I was a young Christian, God taught me by means of many difficult situations to trust in Him and pray for His help. I continued in the school of obedience, sometimes arguing with the Lord and defending my own views with vehement explanations and counter arguments. But at the finals, I always saw I had been wrong and realized I should live continually under God's guidance. Then my praise was overflowing. The inner voice, which I believe is of God, taught me the faithfulness of God![13]

In 1986, when Kaarlo told Ken Crowell and Daniel Yahav the Lord had told him to give Galtronics money to meet payroll and thereby keep the company solvent, he was acting on a leading from God that had been confirmed to him many times previously. In his biography, many examples abound of how he had sensed, then wrestled with God's leading. Here is one example:

> When I was the manager at the Jyvaskyla express office, I went to see my family at Ilmajoki. I had to change trains at Haapamaki. I sat in a small, second-class compartment with the intention of taking a nap. As it happened, a fashionable-looking lady was seated opposite me. I felt irritated for not being able to sit alone after all.
> Then the Lord spoke to me, "Witness to her at once about Christ and salvation in Him."
> "Listen, Lord," I answered. "It's not appropriate for someone to approach another just out of the blue. It's a long way to Seinajoki and I'm quite tired and I wouldn't know how to begin such a conversation. It's not my way to start witnessing so suddenly to anyone at all. Don't you understand, Lord, that people should

<hr>

[13] Ibid, page 21

behave with some courtesy? Who knows, she might get a wrong impression of my intentions since we two are the only ones in this compartment? Not now, Lord. But maybe a little later."

"No," the Lord said. "Right now, start witnessing!"

I left the compartment and walked along the corridor very restlessly thinking how I might begin the conversation and, at the same time, quarreling with my God after receiving such a clear "command." When I returned to the compartment, the lady had a very strange look on her face. Suddenly she gathered her belongings and quickly left the train. I was conscience-stricken. Now my testifying was left undone! Why didn't the lady stay on the train?

The train's departure was delayed and right before we left, the conductor came into the car, pushing the lady in front of him. She then took the same seat she had occupied before. At that moment the Lord told me again, "Now! Right now you are to witness to that lady about Christ and salvation! No more delays!"

How to begin? I thought feverishly. I no longer thought of protesting or disobeying the heavenly voice. Someone had given me an unusual snapshot which was like a picture puzzle. Looking at it carefully, the face of Christ could be seen. As I was praying, I thought of this picture and took it out of my pocket. I said, "Excuse me, ma'am, but I have received a strange picture. Take a look at it. Do you see anyone in it?"

The lady took the picture, turned it around for a while in her hands and then said, "No. I can't see anyone's picture on it."

Then I explained, "This picture had been taken in strange circumstances. A certain woman had planned to commit suicide. She was very depressed and in a hopeless state and couldn't see any other options at that time. She went to the woods where she intended to commit this hopeless act. But the Lord met her there, gave her new faith in life and opened a door to a new hope for living. The act was not done. Later, this lady went back to the same wooded area where she had sensed God giving her new possibilities for life and the courage to conquer life's adversities and trials. She wanted to photograph the spot in the woods where she had earlier been sitting. When the film was developed, it was just like a picture puzzle of Christ's face. Look at it once again."

I showed her the black and white photograph. The shadow of the trees could be seen and, when viewed the right way, one could discern the face of Christ. Now she, too, saw it. She looked at me very seriously and seemed agitated.

"Do you have a habit of talking to strangers this way?" she asked.

"No," I answered. "But immediately when you first came into this compartment, the Lord encouraged me to tell you about salvation in Christ but, wretch that I am, I did not obey. As you may remember, I left the compartment and argued with the Lord that it was not appropriate to witness so suddenly to a perfect stranger."

Tears came to the woman's eyes. "Can you guess why I left this compartment a while ago?"

"No," I replied.

"My husband and I have decided to get a divorce. We cannot live together any longer. Too many things separate us. Nothing unites us anymore. It is impossible to forgive and to ask forgiveness. The only option I could see was to retire from the struggles of life.

"I bought a one-way train ticket so that I may be alone awhile and I bought it for a second-class seat. In my handbag are enough poison tablets for me to end my life. I planned to take the poison right after leaving Haapamaki but I felt irritated because you were in this same compartment hindering my plan. If I had swallowed the tablets here, I wouldn't have been allowed to die in peace because other people were nearby. I was thinking of what I should do. Then, realizing the train had not left yet, I worried maybe the pills wouldn't work fast enough. Maybe it would be very painful. A voice advised me, 'the train hasn't left yet. Go quickly and leave your belongings down at the entrance of the railway car, then go outside and put your head on the rail next to the wheel. It won't take more than a half meter's turn of the wheel to go over your neck and it is done.'

"That is just what I did. I went under the train and waited for it to leave with my neck on the tracks. The conductor stepped off the train right at the moment, saw me bending down under the car and thought I had dropped something there. He took hold of me where he could grab me most quickly and pulled me out from under the train. 'Dear lady, the train is about to leave. You are in great danger!' he said. 'Quickly now, out of there and back to the car!'"

Of course, the conductor didn't understand the lady was purposely under the car and was attempting to commit suicide. He had unwittingly saved the lady's life. We had time to talk. In the best way I knew, I told her Christ is able to repair our broken lives. He can clear up all our marriage problems if we first accept Him as our own Savior and Deliverer. He gives us a new life. Our sins will be forgiven and our hearts will get a peace that lasts throughout all of life's vicissitudes.

Finally, I told her very earnestly, "Go home again. Tell your husband how miraculously God saved your life. Ask one another for forgiveness and forgive one another. You will have a rich life waiting for you. As a born-again person, you will be able to adjust to life's many problems in a new way. You can guide many people who are without hope to know the same Christ to whom, by God's grace, I have tried to lead you. I will pray for you continuously."

The lady had only a one-way ticket to Seinajoki where she had planned to end her life. The situation, however, was changed. At the Seinajoki station I went along to buy her a return ticket to Helsinki and said farewell to her at the steps of the railroad car. This former suicide candidate left to begin a new life.

For my part, I was overwhelmingly grateful to God I had finally listened and obeyed His command to witness to my fellow traveler about the options for a new life. It would have been most dreadful to see her headless body had the train moved. What kind of self-accusations would have haunted me throughout my life! The train would stop and everyone would have viewed the scene of that tragedy.

On that same trip, another strange thing happened. As the train approached Vesanka, I was extremely tired. Vesanka is the first station from Jyvaskyla toward Haapamaki. I was sleeping in the first passenger car. Suddenly I woke up. It was as if an angel had awakened me and an inner voice said, "Out of the train quickly! Hurry!" At least I had learned enough to obey this sudden command. I went without delay to the platform. A railroad siding for a second train was there. The passenger train was waiting for the arrival of a freight train but the switch for the siding had not been turned. The freight train was coming at a fast speed on the same tracks where our train had stopped!

I perceived the danger firsthand and called to God in a loud voice; "Dear Heavenly Father, help us now so there won't be a terrible crash which could bring death to many people!"

The engineer of the passenger train noticed the danger and the train's shrill whistle filled the air. At the same moment, the engineer of the freight train also saw the danger and threw on all the brakes and, with screeching wheels, the freight train stopped barely a meter from the locomotive of our passenger train!

When I arrived home, my wife, Maire, asked me where I was last evening at such and such a time. "I was sleeping on the train at the Vesanka station," I answered.

She asked, "Did anything unusual happen to you?"

"Yes," I replied. "Death was close to me and many others."

Then Maire shared with me; "I felt great distress concerning you at that time. I prayed, 'Lord, help Kaarlo if he is in mortal danger.[14]'"

Within Christendom, there are many different viewpoints and experiences regarding how the Lord Jesus speaks or doesn't speak to His people. Some of you will have read these vignettes from the life of Kaarlo Syvanto and be saying, "Praise the Lord!" Others will have read them and be saying, "No way."

I have had the privilege of making friends with many people who have held different positions on this issue. Some are very comfortable with the type of leading described by Kaarlo while others are skeptical. However, I have never met a person seeking to walk with Jesus who wouldn't agree God does communicate His will to us as His children in a way we can understand and obey. As believers, the Holy Spirit dwells within us. In the fourteenth chapter of John, verses 16 and 17, we are

[14] Ibid, page 39-46

assured that the Father will give us the Spirit of truth in the form of another Counselor who will be with us forever.

It is beyond the scope of this book to deal with this topic of how God leads and/or speaks to his people. My purpose for including this chapter on Kaarlo is not to convince my readers that God wants to speak to you in the way Kaarlo experienced or in any way in particular. I am convinced we must each come to these conclusions ourselves as God leads us. Rather, my purpose is to give you some insight into the background of Kaarlo Syvanto, a person God used in an amazing way to keep Galtronics alive by giving money to meet the payroll. Otherwise, the company would surely have gone under as a business.

Also, as you can see, Kaarlo himself had a ministry through his business contacts.

I have talked about Kaarlo's job as a railroad manager. In 1944, he received a call from the Lord to go to Palestine and minister to the Jews. As he related his call to Palestine, he emphasized, "One shouldn't blindly trust all visions, revelations or callings. One should approach them with certain reservations and they must be studied in the light of God's Word." He gives illustrations of how, over a period of time, his call was confirmed through Scripture and how the Lord prepared him for service.

Kaarlo resigned his position with the railroad in October 1944. From then until 1947, he worked and studied with a mission agency in Finland. We know his family still had the farm they had purchased but we don't know how he supported his family during these years of training. We catch a brief glimpse in the following excerpt:

We still had the country farm at Kintaus and our neighbor there was a farmer named Rajala. He had many children. He came over to chat with me and explained it wasn't possible to make a living on his small farm because it didn't have enough cow pasture. "Couldn't you sell me a small part of your land," he asked, "so that I could make a suitable farm out of this small one?"

I sold him a 17-hectare plot and the farmer was very satisfied. Then a certain Karelian man came to see me. He had a different kind of problem.

"See here, they gave me some land at Muurame as a remuneration for that which I lost in Karelia." The land lost had to do with some of the activities of the Finnish government in dealing with the impact of refugees from World War II. Apparently, this man had some land taken from him, condemnation would be the term used today, and was given property less desirable to him.

"There isn't even a lake nearby. You have a nice place here on the lakeshore. Is there any chance you might exchange farms with me?"

We agreed to that and made a deal for the exchange. As a result, we got in Muurame a larger farm of 56 hectares, of which sixteen were in cultivation. He got our smaller farm at Kintaus with lakeshore and forest. He was delighted to make the exchange. Thus I practiced a kind of emergency settlement; selling to the farmer the extra land he needed and helping the evacuated farmer to get the farm that he liked! We still had the land at Muurame, the Liuskala Farm, which was large in size, with good valuable forest, although the condition of the buildings was inferior.

While I was studying at Larsmo, I received a call to go to the meeting of the Land Redemption Council. This was a government committee responsible after the war for disposition of land. In the meeting with the Council, I was asked if it were true that I was planning to go overseas to work on a mission field. I answered in the affirmative. Then the chairman asked, "How long do you plan to stay there?"

I replied, "The rest of my life!"

He asked, "Is that so? And your family, do you have a family?"

"A wife and four children."

"Well, will they stay to take care of the farm when you leave?"

"They wouldn't stay here," I answered. "They will come later, as soon as they can."

"We need land now for the Karelians. You won't be able to get permission to leave the country as long as this matter remains unfinished."

"Well, let's clear this up as soon as possible," I replied.

They asked me to leave the room for a while and when I returned they said, "You can sell your farm voluntarily to the state if you wish. But to tell the truth, the state won't be able to pay you for at least ten years. We are fixing the price of your farm at 200,000 marks, 2,000 in today's 1980's marks. Here is the deed of sale. Sign your name below."

I had already secured Maire's proxy just in case it would be needed so, with a few strokes of the pen, the entire farm was sold, 56 hectares, 112 acres, of which sixteen were in cultivation. In addition, it had good forestland only 14 kilometers from the city of Jyvaskyla. The Lord gave me great inner joy and peace in this matter. I shook hands with the surveyor as I thanked him and wished him God's blessing in his task of acquiring farms for the Karelians who had lost theirs.

He looked at me in amazement and said, "It's most unusual to leave like this. Usually landowners are swearing as they leave this board meeting!"

But I was able to experience in a marvelous way the truth the writer of the Epistle to the Hebrews states in the tenth chapter: "...and took joyfully the spoiling of your goods, knowing in yourselves that ye have in heaven a better and an enduring substance." That is the mercy and faithfulness of the Lord. It has remained constant to this day and continues on and on.

The chairman of the Land Redemption Council had written about our case to the Farm Administration from whom, somewhat later, came the following reply: "Your case appears to be a special one. The surveyor has recommended that you be paid at least a part of the purchase price now in cash. You will be receiving 70,000 marks immediately even though the payment really should not be made until ten years from now."

In this way the Lord gave us a little money so we might be able to come to Israel. The rest was eaten up by inflation.

Before looking into how Kaarlo and his family arrived in Israel, I would like to reflect on what principles we can learn from his life up to that point. We can see the Lord used adversity to bring good in his life. Even though his natural mother had died and his stepmother neither loved him nor supported the idea of his going to college, the Lord opened the way for him to attend the management training program of the railroad and to secure a job.

Then we saw how temptation came in the form of the offer of bribes by the lumber company. It would have been easy to rationalize because everyone else was doing it and certainly it was more difficult to live on the salary of the railroad. Yet Kaarlo stood for righteousness and helped ferret out corruption even at great personal risk. He was given victory in that effort. Those in leadership who were involved in the corruption suffered ultimate economic reversals and other material effects.

Kaarlo testified that his good fortune in buying a cabin on a lake and being able ultimately to buy a farm with a forest were gifts from the Lord. Then, to see his forest net him significant income while others were taking loses was a clear blessing of God. Again, here was another event tied to his having done the right thing.

Yet, when his own financial gain was, to a large degree, later reversed, and he was left with only enough money to get to Israel and meet his immediate needs, he was not bitter. He did not get angry with those in government service who caused, on a human level, his problems. Rather, he trusted Christ through it all. He had learned the lesson described by the writer of Hebrews 13:5: "Keep your lives free from the love of money and be content with what you have, because God has said, 'Never will I leave you; never will I forsake you.'"

Thus, in many respects, his life mirrored Ken Crowell's as to the lessons the Lord was teaching him about walking in faith and obedience. Money is only a vehicle to accomplish the objective. God will provide what is needed.

Kaarlo learned to view his work as a place where he lived out his Christianity. He was a man of prayer and he prayed about every aspect of his work. His biography shows a man with a very integrated life where faith and work were in no way separated and where no secular vs. spiritual dichotomy existed. Perhaps this personal commitment was the vehicle for his seeing God's purposes for Galtronics and for having no reservations about giving the Lord's resources to help the company survive. He said he gave the money because he had heard the Lord speak to him and he was acting in obedience. He had learned to discern this voice of God in his early years in Finland. Hearing the Lord speak to them in some way was a common thread in every one of the believers' testimonies in the Galtronics story. Although the details varied greatly, each was somehow impacted by the voice of the Lord and was compelled to follow that voice.

It was as Jesus said in John 10:14-16: "I am the good shepherd; I know my sheep and my sheep know me - just as the Father knows me and I know the Father - and I lay down my life for the sheep. I have other sheep that are not of this sheep pen. I must bring them also. They too will listen to my voice, and there shall be one flock and one shepherd."

The manner in which the Good Shepherd got the attention of the sheep varied. The way the Shepherd led the sheep varied. But the constancy of the Shepherd's care and purpose, as well as His goodness, never varied.

Kaarlo ended up going to Palestine in 1947 for a short period. After war broke out in 1948 he returned to Europe to await the time when he could return with his family. Finally, after this delay, he arrived in Israel and supported himself as an agricultural laborer working for a Jewish family that owned a small farm. His main mission became the importing of Bibles into the country. He founded a Bible Society and was responsible for the printing, importation and distribution of hundreds of thousands of Hebrew Bibles that contained both the Old and New Testaments. He did many other works of mercy and led many to Christ. His granddaughter's marriage to Daniel Yahav led him to be intimately acquainted with Galtronics.

It is important to note Kaarlo's belief that Galtronics' mission was primarily given by God for His Kingdom-building purposes and not merely for a commercial venture. It was for this reason Kaarlo gave the money. "The Lord told me to give this to you," he told Ken. Later, the very month Galtronics had a breakthrough financially, he told Ken, "The Lord told me to stop." Ken, Margie, Daniel and the others were enabled to keep the factory open because Kaarlo obeyed what he understood to be God's voice. Ultimately, Israel was blessed because of this obedience. You can obtain the biography of Kaarlo through the John Haller Institute, www.johnhallerinstitute.org.

Chapter Six

A Tool For Integration

Change is a part of life and must be faced regularly. Owners, managers and employees of businesses must accept, adapt to and take advantage of change in order to survive and prosper. But there are periods in the life cycle of a business when major shifts in structure amount to quantum leaps, hopefully forward but sometimes backward. It has been said when a structure, be it a business, church or organization, doubles in size, all of the major systems by which it is managed must grow in tandem for that entity to survive.

In the late 1980's and throughout the 1990's, Galtronics experienced tremendous growth which compelled significant restructuring and transitions in company policies and practices. When a company is small, the entrepreneur can stay in close relationship with all personnel and communications can occur on an informal basis. However, as the business grows, its communication methods must become more formal and systematic to remain effective. This principle is true of both general communication between supervisors and employees and of more encompassing activities such as strategic planning, budgeting, quality improvement, etc.

As people are added within an organization, the number of relationships grows exponentially. Two people have one relationship. Three people enjoy three relationships. But when a fourth person joins, six relationships result concurrently. Each of these relationships must be managed. Initially, many of the people added are production people doing a specific job. Communications in this setting are often one-way, top down, and therefore not very complex. In recent years more emphasis has been placed on listening to the production people and fostering two-way communication. Still, when the business is small with few people, the processes are fairly simple and communications tend to be straightforward.

As a business grows and develops, complexity increases.[15] More new people must connect with the common purpose of the business. Appropriate division of labor decisions must be made so that roles are clear and the people/position fit is maximized. Work processes demand interdependency among people and require cooperation. In fact, the business' effectiveness is directly proportional to the degree of cooperation management is able to achieve.

In an ever more competitive environment this cooperation must result in process improvement so quality continues to go up as prices, lead times and costs continue to go down. The whole issue of improving processes through empowerment of employees necessitates much more dynamic communications.

Pat MacMillan[16] is a leading management consultant in the area of team-building and organizational development. Pat lists good communication as one of the six characteristics of an effective team[17] and an essential element of cooperation. He also says a primary function of leadership is to provide a structure for cooperation, a structure in which all of the players on the team are able to communicate effectively.

Therefore, as a company grows, it becomes impossible for the

[15] How does management determine how fast a business should grow? Is this growth rate something management can control or is it something beyond their control? These are questions that must be wrestled with. Many books have been written on the topic. I will just say that if a business isn't growing, it's probably dying. It is very difficult to stay static. Initially a business begins with one or two customers and one major market. As it grows, there is greater security in multiple customers and multiple markets. This drives growth. Also, if a business has customers who have needs that could be met by someone else, the business can actually grow their own competition if they don't seek to meet their customer's needs. For these and other reasons, growth is inevitable and must be managed.

[16] Pat has a business/ministry by the name of Team Resources in Atlanta and does international consulting with some of the biggest and best for profit and not for profit organizations in the world. His material on Team Building has been a major component of my own management portfolio for the last 15 years. I would recommend it highly.

[17] The six Characteristics Of An Effective Team are: 1.Alignment toward a Common Purpose - which is to accomplish more together than we can alone; 2.Appropriate Division Of Labor - which creates interdependence and demands cooperation; 3.Accepted Leadership - which provides the structure for cooperation; 4.Agreement on the Plan - which provides the process for cooperation; 5.Solid Relationships - which provide the climate for cooperation; 6.Good Communication - which provides the means of cooperation.

entrepreneur to be the central figure in all relationships. He or she must put management in place and work through it. The selection of effective management and the delegation to it of leadership and authority, while maintaining ultimate responsibility for what goes on, is one of the most challenging and critical tasks the entrepreneur faces in business. Every employee must clearly understand the purpose and vision of the company. Each must know his or her role in the overall strategy.

This communication is a challenge when everyone in the company speaks the same language and has the same cultural background. Adding different cultures, languages, geographic regions, a ministry agenda and theological differences presents Goliath-sized challenges to good communication. Also, as first generation leadership begins to phase out, succession planning adds even more to the complexity.

In the case of the inception of Galtronics, Ken and Margie foresaw turning over leadership to Israeli nationals. They had prayed for God to raise up this leadership and had selected and groomed Daniel Yahav, a young man they thought the Lord had presented to them. Ken believed Daniel was not only the best person to work with him on the management team in the 1980's, but also the man to take over as Ken would step out of leadership. As it worked out, this expectation did not prove to be the case. Ken likes to say jokingly, "I spent ten years grooming Daniel for leading the company and then God had to go and ruin it!"

The "problem" occurred when Daniel received a different call from the Lord. That call was to become the full-time pastor of the Peniel Fellowship, the Messianic Fellowship that had been planted by Ken, Margie and others. In 1993, having seen so much growth in both the business and the church, Daniel came to believe he could not do both. Whether the business or the church, he must choose his focus. Daniel sensed God's leading in this new direction. The church was struggling because it did not have a full-time pastor. The elders and the body affirmed this need as well as Daniel's suitability for the position. Ken also wholeheartedly affirmed this decision because he realized this move by Daniel would continue to fulfill his own vision for Israel.

By the early 1990's, Galtronics' sales had grown to almost twenty million dollars. The company was being forced into a global economy. Ken and Margie had known their call was to Israel yet they also knew their Master's call to the church universal was to see the Good News taken to every tribe, tongue and ethnic group. In 1989, Ken did a videotaped interview with Jim Hardie of Marketplace Publishing. In this interview, which was to be shown to churches and schools back in the United States, Ken had issued a call for men and women to replicate in other countries what God had done in Israel through the Gal Group of companies. He offered to help those who answered this call, but emphasized his personal call was to stay focused on Israel.

Ken painted a word picture of what he hoped would happen. He encouraged existing businesses in the United States, perhaps "a manufacturing plant in Washington State," he said, to identify products or services they could produce or sell in countries where most of the unreached people live. Then Ken suggested this U.S. company could recruit a small team of several families, train them in operations, get a prototype operation up and going and then move the prototype to the target country. Ken said he would be willing to assist in these efforts in whatever way he was able without compromising what he perceived to be his call in Israel.

Two years later, in 1991, Sadaam Hussein invaded Kuwait, ushering in Operation Desert Storm. Israel came under attack by Iraq's Scud missiles and suddenly Motorola and other customers of Galtronics came to the realization their chief supplier of cellular phone antennas was vulnerable and susceptible to being shut down. These customers sent a clear message to Ken that if Galtronics wanted to keep their business, it would need to set up plants in Europe, the United States and Asia. Within a few years, Galtronics had five manufacturing sites of varying sizes and levels of production. Ken had wanted to multiply and reproduce similar ventures globally but struggled to be true to his original call to Israel. The Lord had now made Galtronics a truly global player.

By 1996, Galtronics had two plants in Israel, one is in Scotland, one in Georgia in the U.S. and one in Tianjin, China. Just as God had used the earthly plans of Nebuchadnezzar centuries before to accomplish His greater plan, so He used the earthly plans of Sadaam Hussein to accomplish His greater plan at this time. Ken and Galtronics wrestled with the opportunity to use this now global business as a platform for a church planting ministry, to replicate in other countries and among people groups what they had seen God make a reality (verity) in Israel.

As the plans were made for opening the plant in China, Ken, his board, and the management team integrated their missions vision with their business strategy for a win/win approach. Namely, they located the plant where it could be used for a church planting ministry among a target people group whom they knew had little opportunity to hear about Jesus. In this new phase of its life cycle, the company began to realize broader opportunities for integration of faith and work. Growth brought many more opportunities for making disciples and money. It also brought many new challenges.

It is beyond the scope of this book to trace the Galtronics story through the 1990's and into the 21st Century. From what has been previously related however, it is evident as a company passes through various phases of its life cycle, its approach to integration must change. The John Haller Institute has developed a tool for helping believers in a business analyze where that business is in its Integration Life Cycle.[18] This tool seeks to identify differences in how business and Christianity can be integrated. Believers who love Jesus view business differently and these different perspectives can lead to many different conclusions, impacting the way a business is run. As business leaders make decisions about bringing new people into their companies as leaders and even as co-owners, it is vital for all parties to understand their respective views on integrating faith and work. We refer to this integration in terms of a life cycle because the integration approach changes and evolves as the business grows.

In this taxonomy, businesses are described in terms of six different categories: Precarious, Propagation, Presence, Purity, Pluralistic and Pagan.

---

[18] We use the term life cycle here somewhat differently than one usually views the life cycle of a business. We are not talking about product life cycles, but rather it's integration life cycle. This will become more apparent as you read on.

Taxonomy Of Business & Ministry Interaction

Type Of Company	Values Driven By:	Ownership:	Financial Position:	Business Strategy Driven By:	Personal Kingdom Builder Approach Required:
Precarious Company	Evangelical Interpretation To Scriptural Principles. Commitment to living out these principles in business.	Owned by Christians who are firmly committed to furthering the Kingdom Of God through business activities even if the business itself is not financially viable.	Business too risky to set a reasonable rate of return commensurate to the risk. Funding may be donation based or investments with no expected return.	Primarily driven by missions goals and strategy.	Can be overtly open and guided by the Holy Spirit; i.e. free to follow leading without considering financial implications unless donors would disapprove.
Propagation Company	Evangelical Interpretation to Scriptural Principles. Commitment to living out these principles in business.	Owned by Christians who are firmly committed to furthering the Kingdom Of God through business activities but want to make sure the business is financially viable.	Expected return may vary from a rate commensurate with risk or lower if investors are willing. In any case a return on investment is expected.	Dual focus driven by both business financial considerations and missions strategy.	Can be overtly guided by the Holy Spirit; i.e. free to follow leading but also give consideration to practical financial implications of decisions.
Presence Company	Evangelical Interpretation To Scriptural Principles. Commitment to living out these principles in business.	Owned by Christians who are firmly committed to furthering the Kingdom Of God. However they want to do any witnessing type ministry outside the business context. Also they run the business in a way to insure financial viability.	Usually return would be expected to be commensurate with risk. Some might view the risk as lower because overt evangelism or discipleship not taking place.	Driven primarily by financial considerations unless Biblical values are going to by compromised.	Usually have to be more careful about using the name of Jesus. Witnessing approach primarily through life style.
Purity Company	High Ethical Values. Usually accept the 10 commandments along with the Golden Rule. Donít deal with the rest of Scriptures in business context.	Owned by individuals who believe business should be run according to Judeo/Christian values.	Risk governed by normal market forces and expectations.	Driven primarily by financial considerations unless ethical values are going to be compromised.	Usually have to be more careful about using the name of Jesus. Witnessing approach primarily through life style.
Pluralistic Company	Culturally driven by predominantly accepted values of society. Often times this is "fuzzy" and shifts over time. Pragmatic dollar orientation.	Owned by individuals who do not believe personal religious beliefs should impact business; or whose actions would indicate they believe this.	Risk governed by normal market forces and expectations.	Driven primarily by financial considerations unless legal issues are going to be compromised. Sometimes this is pushed to the limit.	Must be very careful about bringing up spiritual matters at all. May be extreme pressure to compromise family or other values.
Pagan Company	Driven primarily to make money and to accomplish other objectives.	Owned by individuals who are aligned with evil powers and principalities.	Risk governed by normal market forces but may make decisions consulting mediums, etc.	Driven by financial considerations or other objectives.	Should get out unless called. Spiritual warfare expected.

All businesses in their early stages of life are Precarious. In the integration life cycle, we are using the term with more specificity. Viewing the business as a means of furthering Christ's Kingdom will often create occasions when the business would be started even when there was not a reasonable probability it would make money for a significant period of time. If one were looking to the business only as a source of making money and not of making disciples, he would not start the business. But when the primary purpose or mandate he is seeking is making disciples, he may very well begin the business knowing he will have to inject money into it for a longer time frame until it can become self-supporting. It is this stage we refer to as Precarious.

When the business reaches the point where it breaks even and its owners are committed to pursuing both the making of money and the making of disciples, we refer to that as being a Propagation company. Proactive planning and implementation toward both objectives is a necessary factor for the business to fall into this category.

As a company grows and begins to hire more and more non-Christians or Christians who are not committed to making disciples, it begins to move into the Presence stage. Integrating Biblical principles into the warp and woof of the business makes sense to many who would be uncomfortable with what they would view as proselytizing, defined by Webster as "to induce someone to convert to one's faith; to recruit someone to join one's party, institution, or cause; to recruit or convert especially to a new faith, institution, or cause."

In talking about his ministry in Troas of preaching the gospel of Christ, Paul said in II Corinthians 2:12-17 that some found his message a sweet fragrance while others found it a smell of death. No matter how relationally sensitive we are, the exclusivity of the gospel can be offensive to those who reject God's way and this view can make some uncomfortable, believers and unbelievers alike.

When it comes to Christianity, a fairly small number of believers are committed enough to the making of disciples to wholeheartedly support the use of the company they are working with to accomplish this goal. Let's face it. We live in a day and age when tolerance is a highly-touted value, and this cultural pressure for tolerance can lead to even more discomfort on the part of those who want to be accepted. This can make the line between a Propagation company and a Presence company a distinct one.

Because of this line, as a company grows and more people come into the employment ranks, conflict often begins to develop for business owner or leader. As the leader moves to create opportunities for advancement for all employees, the likelihood increases that people will be placed in leadership who are not committed to, and may often be resistant to, the goal of making-disciples. As time goes on, other aspects of the Bible become offensive. A continual pressure or force moves the company toward secularism. Eventually, a company will move from a Presence stage to a Purity stage. Here, the Ten Commandments or the "golden rule" of doing unto others as you would have them do unto you becomes the essence of spiritual values within the company, a movement generally supported by both religious and nonreligious people except perhaps those committed to a strict and rigid belief in "separation of church and state."

In recent years in the United States, there have been strong efforts on the part of some to remove all mention of the Ten Commandments from every area of life. This trend will make it more likely businesses will move from the Purity stage to the Pluralistic stage in which spiritual matters may be addressed only very cautiously if at all.

Is this movement inevitable? Can a business led or owned by those committed to World Evangelization move in the upstream direction against this current? How do followers of Jesus, who want to obey Christ by seeking to make disciples, live for Him in these different types of companies? These are the types of questions for which The John Haller Institute is seeking answers.

It is most difficult for a follower of Jesus to work within what is referred to in the Taxonomy as a Pagan company. Owners and/or leaders in this type of company are actively involved in activities that link them and their business with demonic forces. A friend of mine worked in a company where the owners consulted a medium for guidance on business decisions. It is unknown how many of these situations may exist. I know of a large company that has held séances for their board of directors. Others promote yoga or various forms of meditation for their employees. Obviously there is some subjectivity in making these assessments. Yet great discernment is needed by Christians who discover these types of activities within the company where they are working. It may be that a Christian needs a specific call from God to work within this type of company.

As you take some time to look over this matrix and become familiar with the distinctive elements of these six different types of companies, you will recognize that hard and fast lines don't divide them. Rather, they are meant to be helpful descriptive terms to aid those seeking to have a ministry by increasing understanding of the business reality and helping to determine how to be effective in that context. Believers can have a ministry of serving Christ and furthering His Kingdom in each of these business types. However, the approach believers take must fit the type of company where they are working.

Ken and Margie saw Galtronics as a company owned by the Lord Jesus and dedicated to furthering His Kingdom. They repeatedly told me, "This is God's business. If He wants it to survive, it will. If He wants it to go bankrupt, it will. We are here to serve Him."

On another occasion, Ken stressed to me believers should not look at developing missionary companies for anticipated financial gain. "They may make money, but they may not. Their goal should be to obey Christ."

Ken and Margie were willing to accept donated support from Kaarlo Syvanto. As we said earlier, Kaarlo was convinced Galtronics was of God and its success was vital to Israel. For this reason, he felt motivated to donate money to Galtronics.

As Ken brought in leaders and investors he found they did not always share the same view about how to integrate Christianity and Christ's mandate to make disciples into the business.

Alignment toward a common purpose is another of business consultant Pat MacMillan's critical requirements in achieving synergy from a team. If an owner of a business wants to align the purpose of that business with what he perceives as Christ's purpose, but a leader to whom the owner is delegating authority does not share that sense of alignment, it can cause problems. The same is true if an outside investor is brought into the business.

Another characteristics of an effective team according to MacMillan is agreed upon strategy. Christians can have different viewpoints on how to obey Christ's disciple-making mandate. Those leaning more toward a Purity or Presence approach are often likely to take money generated from the business and give it to not-for-profit entities or individuals who are actively pursuing Kingdom goals instead of using company personnel and time to pursue these goals themselves.

It must be understood that even two people wanting to operate a Propagation business can differ as to strategy. As was earlier mentioned, these categories are not hard and fast but should be viewed more as points on a continuum. The purpose for considering them is to promote discussion and help create better alignment between those who are working together or thinking of working together. By directly addressing differing view, conflicts can be avoided. If a disagreement surfaces, this taxonomy can be used as a tool to diagnose where the differences lie and to help facilitate a resolution.

When Ken and Margie sought to turn over authority to others, they had varying results. I was told by some middle managers in the company that a "glass ceiling" existed, above which no non-Christian could advance. While this may be viewed as a negative thing, the fact is there are many privately held companies in which one has to be a member of the immediate family to be in top leadership positions. This practice, known as nepotism, is not discrimination.

In the 1970's, a group published the New Testament in a popular version that carried the subtitle, "Letters To Street Christians in God's Forever Family." The Body of Christ is a "forever family," therefore it makes sense that some would want to keep leadership positions in their company "in the family" to better insure loyalty to the purpose and values distinctive to believers in Jesus.

So again we ask, why even concern oneself about these things? Why not keep your company totally secular? The main reason can be summed up in the word, "love." If we love Jesus and know He loves every man, woman and child in the world, we are motivated by that love to tell others about it. Therefore, we want to avail ourselves of every vehicle possible to make known God's love. Business offers a strategic vehicle for doing just that.

In the years ahead, the John Haller Institute hopes to publish many other case studies about businesses in which Christians have sought to integrate their faith and business. Some of these will be motivational. Others may take specific issues and seek to describe how these issues were dealt with or how they might have been dealt with differently.

If you know of a business you'd like to read about, please contact us. We'd love to pursue it. In the meantime, wherever you are, in whatever type of company you find yourself, we encourage you to follow the leading of the Lord to do all you can to make disciples.

As believers today seek to further the Kingdom of God and find and fulfill their ministry, the structure in which they work may very well provide important opportunities for that ministry. The Bible talks about 'ministry" as the role of a servant for Christ's sake. In our day, we have come to associate the term "ministry" with paid professional clergy, thus creating an artificial distinction between clergy and laity.

One of the hallmarks of the Protestant Reformation was emergence of a principle known as "The Priesthood of All Believers" whereby reformers asserted all believers stand as equals before God, all with gifts of serving in some capacity and all with equal responsibility to do so. This was in contrast to "clericalism," a view held by the Holy Roman Catholic Church and one, which claimed clergy, had a special, more important relationship with God than the masses.

Today most Protestants' view of ministry and ministers is more closely parallel to the still prominent Catholic view of clericalism than to what is taught by the Protestant Reformers about all believers serving equally but in different roles.

The Protestant Reformers' view of ministry was largely shaped by their interpretation of key Pauline passages such as Ephesians 4:11-13 where we read, "The gifts he [Jesus] gave were that some would be apostles, some prophets, some evangelists, some pastors and teachers; to equip the saints for the work of ministry, for building up the body of Christ, until all of us come to the unity of the faith and of the knowledge of the Son of God, to maturity, to the measure of the full stature of Christ."

Christ has given those who are gifted and called to be pastors and teachers a role to equip all believers for works of ministry. Compare, for a moment, this equipping responsibility to the job of an athletic team coach:

They could hardly believe they had been able to get tickets. The last game of the NCAA basketball championship series and here they were, seated on the half court line, five rows up. The whole arena was alive with energy as the teams warmed up. The referees were conferring at one end of the court when suddenly something unbelievable occurred! The players, dressed in their warm ups, began to file off the court and climb up into the stands, finding seats throughout the crowd. What on earth was going on? The air of disbelief spread and a deathly silence fell upon the building. Then something else occurred that caused a murmur from the crowd. As realization of what was happening grew, the murmur turned to laughter. The laughter gave way to heckling and jeering and finally booing as people began to shout, "We want our money back!" The coaches had put on tennis shoes and had begun to play half court, three on three, as the players and fans alike looked on.

Fanciful story? No doubt. Yet there is a certain parallel to reality in the Church of Jesus Christ today. Let's take a look at the parallels and come to a conclusion. While we don't know a great deal about the supernatural world that lies beyond the veil of what we can see, hear, smell, taste and touch, we do know some things. We know in the heavenly realm there are powers and principalities watching what is happening on earth as God works out His plan through his Church.

These entities are divided into two camps. One group is in submission to the Father and is committed to glorifying Him in all they do. The other group is in rebellion against the Father and is seeking to undermine His will. Men and women, boys and girls, here on earth are also involved. God has created them with a freedom to choose. In His infinite power, He could easily force every creature to bow down and worship Him. He could compel us to love Him. Yet, in His love, this demand would be a violation of His character. Instead, He has given us a freedom to choose and proven we are significant individually to Him because He has given each of us a choice either to seek relationship with Him or to reject Him.

So what does all this have to do with our basketball analogy? Each individual in the Body of Christ has been given at least one gift and with it comes an expectation to serve. The primary role of pastors is to equip believers for service or ministry. They are to use their gifts to serve as coaches so the saints can be active participants in the church and in the world. Unfortunately, most pastors would admit too often they end up doing the ministry for the saints instead of preparing the saints for ministry. The coaches have put on their tennis shoes and are on the court as the saints sit in the stands and watch.

Has the Church ever really succeeded in making the switch from clericalism to "The Priesthood of All Believers?" Today if believers were to experience an occasion such as described earlier at a Final Four championship, they would be shocked and would clamor for their money back. Yet they readily buy in to the view that professionals "called" to full time, paid service are the true ministers while they are mere spectators. What has happened?

I attend a Biblically-based church with an active missions program. Our church of some 1,200 members supports hundreds of missionaries. Every year we have a missions conference at which time the call goes out for people to consider a call to "full time Christian service." I asked a close friend on the missions committee to tell me what he could believe God for in terms of numbers responding to this call. I suggested ten percent. He replied, "Oh no! I would be thrilled with three percent!" That means in 1,200, 36 would be called to respond to God's call to the ministry and full-time Christian service. The other 97% would support them by paying their salaries and cheering them on.

At a recent conference, we had a keynote speaker who was a founder of a very active missions agency. He was in his 70's and had been with the agency for over 50 years. In his effort to motivate more people to come forward in response to the call, he said, "Despite all of the great things God has been doing, we (the Church) keep losing ground. In India alone, one million people are born each month. We are losing ground! If you respond, we may be able to catch up. Please consider fulltime Christian service."

Unfortunately, we didn't get even a 3% response rate that year even though it was a good conference.

We're losing ground. More missionaries are retiring. The population keeps growing. The twelve million per year growth in India computes to only a little over 1% population growth. What can be done?

Albert Einstein once defined insanity as "expecting different results but doing the same things." The point of the axiom is if you expect different results, you have to change your methods. Can we expect to gain ground in missions if we keep the same methods? Can we keep calling for the full time Christian ministers or missionaries to come forth and hope and pray for 3% to respond? What is to be done?

What if we could find a way to reverse the 97% / 3% phenomenon and have instead a 3%/97% result? What if the 3% who are paid full time professionals equipped the 97% full time non-paid believers to serve God through their professions and occupations? Would this not be more in line with Paul's observation of how God intended the Church to function?

By far, the vast majority of the 97% are involved in some way in seeking to earn a living in order to provide for their families and in some way to support the 3%. For this work, they receive a paycheck, which they take to the bank or have it automatically deposited. From this account, they draw money out for various purposes. During the week, they spend 40+ hours in this money-earning mode. In a year's time, they have hundreds, if not thousands of conversations with other people. Here they encounter many unbelievers, many who have never had a significant conversation about who Jesus is. Could not these relationships become a bridge of trust across which the good news about Jesus Christ could be communicated? Could not these believers begin to pray regularly for their co-workers, customers, clients, vendors and suppliers that those who don't know Jesus could come to know Him? Could they not in some cases begin a Bible Study and invite some associates to join them? Might this study not grow into a small group that could provide pastoral care to help these folks apply Biblical principles to their lives and realize the fullness of life that Christ brings?

What is keeping this from happening? What forces cause Christians among both the 3% full-time workers and the 97% paying parishioners to accept as normative these barriers that divide so-called secular from sacred and clergy from laity?

A paradigm is an example that serves as pattern or model. We sometimes consciously, and more often unconsciously, make decisions based on examples of what we see others doing. If all of our examples of piety tell us that all spiritual people become full time Christian workers and raise their support from others who don't feel the call, then that is assumed to be normative and not questioned. Paradigms are very powerful, especially because we don't realize they are operative. What would happen if we could discover examples of men and women who, in the context of their professions and occupations, saw themselves as full-time Christian workers and ministers of the Gospel?

In the 1970's, I read a little paperback book by William Danker entitled, *Profit for The Lord*. This work was an historical study of Moravians and the Basel Mission Trading Company. In his introduction, Danker observes:

Protestant overseas missions in recent times have often demonstrated massive opposition to economic activities, particularly if these were intended to produce income. With uncritical piety, the axiom that the church (and therefore the mission) should have nothing to do with business has been widely accepted as a working presupposition. It was not always so. Early in the history of Protestant missions we find important missionary efforts taking a much more sympathetic view of economic activities. In some cases economic activities became the mainstay of missionary support; in others it provided significant assistance.

Similar perspectives still exist and are hindering world evangelization. Danker proceeds in the rest of his book to give example after example of Christians who sought to integrate their call to Christ with their job or occupation. Not just individuals, but organizations are shaped by their paradigms. Danker shows God can use business structures such as trading companies and manufacturing plants to further His Kingdom. In his review[19] of some of the contributions of the Moravians, Danker makes the following statement:

> But the most important contribution of the Moravians was their emphasis that every Christian is a missionary and should witness through his daily vocation. If other Christians had studied the example of the Moravians more carefully, it is possible that the businessman might have retained his honored place within the expanding Christian world mission beside the preacher, teacher and physician.

The examples people hear about in our missionary conferences are from the people who are raising their own support, the 3%. This pattern perpetuates the paradigm. Again, we are losing ground! What can be done?

An example of a man who integrated his call to follow Christ with his profession was John Haller who is mentioned by William Danker in Profit For The Lord.[20] Haller was a master weaver who went to India from Switzerland in the mid 1800's. He set up a lab and performed research on various materials and dyeing compounds, eventually discovering the process for making Khaki that he then marketed to the local police and to the British armed forces. Haller took the weaving industry from being a cottage industry to a whole new level, importing over 20 looms and

[19] Danker, William; *Profit For The Lord,* Intent, Naperville, Il, 2000
[20] Danker, p.87.

91

providing jobs for hundreds of people. But most of all, his goal was to further the Kingdom of God. He was a business-professional missionary.

In an effort to help find other examples and to better understand how to better equip the saints for the work of the ministry in the context of their daily lives, Monday through Saturday, the John Haller Institute has been formed. The Institute seeks to research examples of individuals and organizations that have sought to integrate business, ministry and missions. For most Christians, these terms are thought of independently. Some even say they cannot be mixed. The John Haller Institute has examples that prove this view is not true. We are seeking to tell these stories so the Church can rediscover "The Priesthood of All Believers" and can not only stop losing ground but also begin to gain ground once again.

It seems the coaches have put on their tennis shoes and gone out on the court to play the game while the players have climbed up into the stands to watch. Ken and Margie Crowell saw their role as players who regard business as a place where ministry happens. As William Danker pointed out, the business person has been much neglected in the world of Christian missions. Thankfully, Ken and Margie saw the potential and acted on it. Many others like them have also been responsive to the call of God to minister for Christ's sake and pursue being disciple-makers in and through their business.

The John Haller Institute is committed to making the stories of these business disciple-makers known. It is our heartfelt hope that as stories are told, others will catch the vision and make even greater strides toward utilizing business as a Kingdom-building vehicle, far beyond just being a means to support not for profit efforts. The John Haller Institute promotes this type of research, discussion and writing. We seek to motivate and instruct by identifying principles of integration that will inspire and equip the saints to be ever more effective in their works of ministry in business.

Chapter Seven

Conclusion

Ken and Margie Crowell are two followers of Jesus who sought to align with His will. Their story is filled with what some would call confusing and contradicting facts but God used them, as He has used thousands of other ordinary people who have sought to obey their extraordinary Lord. And the story goes on. Ken and Margie have never regretted their call to minister through their business. They have seen how God has used this ordinary means to accomplish extraordinary results. Through the struggles and drudgery of everyday commerce, lives have been transformed with eternal consequences. Esther and Gary Hull were both Jews who did not believe in Jesus as the Messiah when they came to work at Galtronics. They met each other there and ended up marrying. Later, they both met Jesus there and found the fulfillment of having their lives transformed by the power of the Holy Spirit. Their story exemplifies the vision Ken and Margie had for the company.

Every Christian has been given the purpose of being a disciple-maker. The main imperative in Jesus' Great Commandment is "make disciples." Going, baptizing and teaching to obey are all gerunds that describe the 'how' of disciple-making. Our professional career is actually a means of going and teaching to obey. Therefore, we must make sure our paradigm of work and career includes this disciple-making purpose or we run the risk of running our life race in vain. We would miss out on the most central elements of what is the essence of the Christian life. Integrating our disciple-making purpose into our professional career can add a whole new sense of purpose and meaning.

After the Fall of Man, recorded in Genesis 3, work has had its cursed elements. Yet even as Jesus can set us free from the eternal effects of the curse by giving us eternal life, just so He can set us free from the effects of the curse in this life as well. In John 10:10 we read Jesus' words: "I have come that they may have life, and have it to the full."

Work will still have its problems but as we view our work as a context of disciple-making and begin to pray for the blessing of Christ on our ministry, a whole new abundance can come to us and, through us, to others around us.

Very few Christians ever think about a business as a structure through which to make disciples and to thereby further the Kingdom of God. They may consider business, ministry and missions as separate realities but they don't relate them.

Ken and Margie did integrate them and saw their ministry in the context of their business as fulfilling their mission and accomplishing God's plan for the Church.

As you read this account of Ken and Margie's pilgrimage, you may not agree on the track that Ken and Margie have taken or you may agree they were led of God. If the latter is true, you may nonetheless think they are the exception to the rule, somehow "cut from a different cloth" than ordinary Christians.

The purpose of relating these events is not to evaluate their business acumen. Rather it is to demonstrate their commitment to Christ and to give the reader some idea of what God was able to do through them because of that commitment.

Our hope and prayer is you will not see them as the exception to the rule or conclude they are in any way different from ordinary people. In our view, it is the very fact an extraordinary God used these obedient ordinary people to accomplish amazing things that make the lessons learned from their story so applicable to others. Again, our hope is you will interpret these events with an eye of faith and you will be encouraged and challenged to consider this type of ministry approach yourself. If you are of that mind, please let us know. We will align you with others who can pray for you and help you in this effort.

If you are open but still have reservations, may I encourage you to keep praying and ask the Lord to direct your steps. The fact remains millions live in countries where traditional missionaries can not get visas, but Christian business professionals can enter with freedom.

Who will go and tell them about Christ's love? Who will demonstrate the reality of the life-changing power of the Gospel?

Pastors, I would encourage you to seek to equip the saints in your congregation for the work of the ministry that their Lord has called them to. Help them discover and use their spiritual gifts. And if they are called to a vocation that has them in a business, please encourage them to view that business as a context for ministry. Encourage them to pray for those with whom they work. Help them to develop effective methods of ministry in the business context.

Businessmen and women, think through the freedom you have and seek to use that freedom to win others to Christ. Ask God to use you to serve and save those around you.

Business Owners, please consider using your business as a vehicle for reaching others with the good news of the Gospel of Jesus Christ. Pursue reaching out to a people group or minister in an area where a financially viable business is not reasonable but where commerce is still a strategic means to form trust relationships, serve and introduce people to Christ. Job creation is a very important need in most areas of the world and relief and development is not an end in itself.

We invite all of you to contact us at the John Haller Institute. We will do all we can to help you move forward. If you have questions or comments about what you have read, please let us know. We trust you have enjoyed this documentary about Ken and Margie Crowell. May God richly bless you in your pilgrimage of faith.